The Brilliant Beaver Guidebook

Ideas and approaches to help you and your group get the most out of Scouting

By James Louttit

With Ideas from Jim O'Carroll and Emily Battle

Illustrated By Tais Krymova

Contents

Introduction

Scouting is amazing! It's fun, it teaches valuable skills and it creates friendships that can last a lifetime. But it can also be quite hard. A lot of Scouters struggle to come up with exciting new programme ideas that keep the meetings and activities fresh and engage all the elements of the programme. This book is mostly about giving you those ideas and helping you to come up with more yourself. I've told a few stories from my experiences along the way, but I hope you'll enjoy it by flicking through it before your planning meeting and picking out ideas that you will customise to your group. If I'm honest, it's also written for that frantic half-hour before the Beaver meeting that we all have from time to time where we just need an idea for what to do with the kids when they turn up full of energy and looking at us wondering what's next.

However you use the ideas in this book, I'd love for you to make them your own. Change them, add to them, throw away parts and replace them with other ideas. Write notes in the margins about what you've done and what did or didn't work about it. Share the ideas with fellow Scouters, take videos of your activities and share them with the kid's parents. You are an incredible inspiring person who gives up their time volunteering for an organisation that does huge amounts of good in the world. Anything I can do to support you, I'd love to do more of, and hopefully this book will be part of that support.

Scouting has been a part of my life for as long as I can remember. My journey started 36 years ago when I first put on the Beaver uniform and learned the "Beaver shout". The thrill of performing my first campfire skit, the sense of achievement on earning my first badge, and the joy of making lifelong friendships are as important today as they were in the 1980s. Perhaps even more so as our kids are under attack by wave after wave of screen-based activity designed by highly paid experts to attract their attention for another click or scroll wherever possible and keep them indoors, away from their friends and the kinds of activities that I'll describe through this book.

Scouting is about interacting with people of all ages, physical activity, learning new skills and pure fun! It grows and develops and changes as generation after generation put their stamp on it, building on old traditions and inventing new ones. The Beaver shout, which I introduced to Castleknock Beavers in 2021 after learning it in High Wycombe in 1986 is now being enjoyed by 25 kids at around 7:15 every Wednesday evening in a sports hall in Diswellstown, just because I remembered it, and thought they might enjoy it one evening so took a few minutes to teach it to them.

If you don't know it, the Beaver shout goes:

1,2,3 who are we?

We are Beavers, can't you see?

B E A, V E R

BEAVERS BEAVERS

RAH RAH RAH

It is best shouted at the top of the voice, and it starts with the kids squatting down and then jumping up for the "rah rah rah" bit. Seeing Joe, Koa, Thomas and the rest of the kids giving it gusto every Wednesday evening is one of the highlights of my week.

From Beavers, I moved on to Cubs, then to Scouts, and finally to Venture Scouts. Each step of the journey introduced me to new challenges, skills, and unforgettable experiences. I built confidence, learned skills and developed friendships that have lasted a lifetime. I was awarded the Queen Scout award at Windsor castle by Lord Baden-Powell's granddaughter, I went on an amazing expedition to the Kandersteg international Scouting centre in Switzerland and completed the "endurance 80" hike on two occasions – walking 80 Km in less than 24 hours and on the second occasion winning the "fastest mixed group to complete" award. That award still sits proudly on a shelf in my living room. The stories and memories I have built from those adventures are amongst the fondest of my life. 3 of my close friends from Scouting flew over to Ireland (where I now live) last Summer to kayak around Lambay Island with me – and the safety boat was crewed by a friend from my new Scouting life in Dublin.

I stayed in touch with my Venture Scout section all through university and when I went on a 2-month expedition to the Danum Valley Nature reserve in Borneo as part of a re-foresting experiment in 2002, I was one of the most well-prepared people in the group – including some of the expedition Leaders! Living in a hammock for two-months, dodging snakes and falling trees, dealing with leeches and biting insects and spending every day doing the back-breaking work of planting hundreds of saplings is some people's idea of hell – but I loved every minute of it! I still have the t-shirt we made as a group, and on the back – amongst all the nicknames that we gave each other over the two months is me – James "Beaver Leader" Louttit.

My adventure didn't stop there. Even after I started my first job in London, I took on the role of Explorer Scout Leader with two of my great Scouting friends and I always made sure that I left the office at 5:30 on a Monday to be back in Loudwater to argue with a bunch of sullen teenagers about why we should do a hike instead of going bowling yet again! I hope my leadership skills have developed since then, and I would be able to inspire and motivate rather than argue, but as a 22 year-old I still had a lot to learn. We ran that section until 2009, when, after meeting the love of my life, I moved to Ireland and got married.

For a few years, my involvement in Scouting took a back seat, but the spirit of Scouting never left me. When my daughter was old enough to join Beavers, I found myself back in the thick of it all, invigorated by her excitement and the nostalgia it invoked. I re-joined the 175th Castleknock Scouts near where I now live as an assistant Beaver Leader. The rest of the leaders in the section were hard-working volunteers, doing an amazing job to make a memorable and engaging programme for the kids. I didn't want to either take on too much responsibility (I had a busy job at the time) or to step on anyone's toes, so I pitched in, helping where I could, teaching knots and compasses at some evenings, but not taking a leading role.

When Steve, the Beaver section leader came to me in 2019 and asked me to run the section, I initially said "no", but after a couple of weeks persuading me, I said I'd try it out.

It was a disaster! I had recently landed a dream job as the Chief Information Officer of a big recruitment company in Dublin, but I was extremely busy fire-fighting and building a team in work. I had no time for Scouting apart from Wednesday nights (which I always prioritised).

Waking up at 3am one morning worrying about the fact that someone had applied for their daughter to join the Beavers and I hadn't replied to the email was the last straw. I emailed Steve and the other leaders there and then and asked them to take back the reins until I could get properly organised. Steve, and his wife Maeve, and their friends Olly and Edel understood and stayed with the section through the next couple of years, all through covid, even though their kids had moved on and left Scouts.

Covid caused us lots of problems, but as it started to ease, and I had managed to get control of my work-life balance by training up and delegating to my team at work, my mind shifted back to becoming a section leader again. I met with the Group Scout Leader – another James – James C, and we started to hatch a succession plan for the group to allow people who had "served their time" and wanted to move on to hand over to another generation of leaders.

As we talked, on evening walks through the Phoenix Park in Dublin, we figured out a plan. We'd ask Emily to take over as Beaver Leader, Cathal would become the Cub Leader, and James C would move away from the Group Leader role and become more active in the Scout Section with Frank. I would take over as Group Scout Leader and try to get a handle on all the admin that is required to run a group, as well as recruiting lots of new leaders to come along, learn and help out.

This plan has largely played out the way that we wanted it to, with one devastating exception. In September 2022, Cathal O'Driscoll, our new Cub Section Leader, father to two of our youth members and a good friend to everyone in the group, passed away suddenly. He was an amazing man, with passion and dedication for Scouting, and he would have been an incredible inspiration to the kids going through our group. We haven't done it yet, but one of Cathal's ideas for raising money for the Scout den that we desperately need was to attempt the Guinness World Record for the World's largest S'More. One day we will make that attempt, but for the moment, this book is dedicated to Cathal's memory and to the memory of people like him in groups all over the world.

Today, I serve as the Group Scout Leader, involved in all sections, from Beavers to Scouts (we lost our Venture unit a few years ago, but we hope to start again next year as we have some really keen Scouts that we think will want to stay on). Over the decades, I've had the privilege of working with remarkable leaders, each with their own unique style, and from whom I've learned many invaluable lessons. As I write this book, my aim is to try to distil the wisdom gleaned from these leaders, share the very best traits and approaches I've seen in action, and hopefully, make your journey as a Beaver Leader not just easier, but also a lot of fun!

Being a Beaver Leader is about more than organising activities and managing a group of young children; it's about shaping lives, sparking curiosity, fostering a love for nature, and instilling the principles of Scouting in the hearts of our youngest members. It's about crafting the kind of experiences that stay with a child for life, much like my own Beaver days still resonate with me.

This book is a collection of ideas, strategies, and practical tips that I've found to be effective over my years in Scouting. My hope is that it will not only help you navigate your journey as a Beaver

Leader but also inspire you to create fun, memorable, and transformative experiences for your Beavers.

Here's to creating the best Beaver experience possible for our kids and everyone else's!

The Essence of Scouting: Principles and Values

Scouting is not just an activity; it's a way of life, a value system that guides young people to grow into responsible, caring, and active citizens. At the heart of Scouting are the Promise and Law, fundamental principles that imbue our Scouts with a strong sense of duty and commitment. These are simplified for Beavers, and ideally will be incorporated into the meetings at the start or the end.

The Beaver Scout Promise

I promise to do my best,
to be a good Beaver Scout,
to love the world, and
to love one another.

The Beaver Scout Law

Beaver Scouts are **friendly**, they always say Hello, Please and Thank You!
Beaver Scouts Are **kind**, they work hard and help their family and friends.

The words are simple, and they form the cornerstone of our values, setting the course for a Scout's journey. If we could all be a bit more friendly and a bit more kind, and have those at the core of our character, wouldn't the world be an even better place! I say "even" better place, because despite all the negativity out there in the news, I believe we live in an amazing world full of incredible people who (almost) always have their hearts in the right place and are trying to do what they believe is best for each other.

This positive outlook, which was instilled by my family as well as my Scouting experiences is another reason why I've had a fairly successful career. Scouting teaches us to see the best in people, and to work with everyone, be inclusive, and see challenges as opportunities to learn. These ideas are powerful, and helpful, and I firmly believe that positive people have happier lives, and that Scouting makes people more positive.

The Scouting framework is designed to nurture and support each Scout's journey. It comprises eight key elements:

Promise and Law: These guiding principles form the backbone of our value system, providing a moral compass for our Scouts as they interact with others and navigate life's challenges.

Personal Progression: We value the journey more than the destination. Every Scout grows at their own pace, achieving milestones in their unique way. Our role is to support this individual growth and to celebrate both personal and team achievements.

Learning by Doing: People learn best through hands-on experience. By undertaking tasks and reflecting on their experiences, children gain not just practical skills but also insights about themselves and their capabilities.

Small Group System: Our structure emphasizes teamwork. Within each section, small teams work together, fostering cooperation, leadership, and personal development.

Symbolic Framework: Stories, traditions, and themes ignite the imagination and facilitate learning. This creative and symbolic framework is shaped as much by the Beavers themselves as by the leaders.

Nature and Outdoors: The great outdoors is our classroom, offering a sense of freedom, challenge, and adventure. Our activities encourage a close connection with nature and an escape from everyday home life.

Young People and Adults Working Together: Scouting is a partnership between young people and adults. While adults provide more guidance in the younger sections, as Scouts grow older, the relationship evolves into a partnership where decision-making is shared.

Service and Commitment: Scouting encourages active citizenship. Scouts engage with their local community, providing service, and committing to making a better world.

Embracing these principles and embedding them into our activities, discussions, and actions is the essence of Scouting. As Beaver Leaders, we can live these values and, by example, inspire our young Beavers to do the same. Whether it's through a simple act of kindness during a camping trip or an elaborate service project, we're guiding our Beavers to become responsible, caring individuals who are ready to make a positive difference in the world.

Understanding Beaver Scouts: Ages 6-8

Ages 6 to 8 are a period of significant growth and development for children, both physically and emotionally. It's a time when they start to explore the world outside of their immediate family and begin to understand their role within a larger community.

At this age, children are full of questions and brimming with an insatiable curiosity about the world around them. They are fascinated by new experiences, whether it's spotting a ladybird on a leaf during a nature walk or creating a paper boat that actually floats. Every activity, every interaction is an opportunity to learn something new, and their enthusiasm can be infectious.

Their view of the world is literal and concrete; they learn best through hands-on experiences and tangible activities. Abstract concepts can be challenging for them, so it's essential to break down big ideas into smaller, manageable parts that they can understand and relate to. Nature and the outdoors become fantastic classrooms, offering endless opportunities for exploration and discovery.

Socially, Beavers are beginning to navigate friendships and group dynamics. They are eager to be part of a team, but they are still learning how to cooperate, share, and resolve conflicts. They can be fiercely competitive one moment and incredibly caring and cooperative the next. They may need guidance to understand and manage their feelings and to empathise with others.

You'll find a variety of personalities in your Beaver group. Some may be outgoing and eager to participate, while others may be quieter and more reserved. Some may love the thrill of adventure, while others might find comfort in routine and predictability. Each child is unique, and recognising and celebrating these differences can create a rich and inclusive environment for all.

At this stage, adult and parental support remains crucial. While Beavers are becoming more independent, they still need the reassurance and guidance of trusted adults. They look to their leaders and parents for approval and validation, and their presence provides a sense of safety and security. Consistent, clear communication between leaders and parents can greatly enhance a Beaver's experience.

Despite their growing independence, Beavers till need clear boundaries and structure. They thrive in environments where expectations are explicit and routines are consistent. They also respond well to positive reinforcement, so recognising their efforts and celebrating their achievements, no matter how small, can boost their self-esteem and motivation.

Understanding the mindset of a Beaver Scout is the first step towards creating a meaningful and enjoyable Scouting experience for them. Our role is not just to guide them through activities, but also to support their overall growth and development. This is a beautiful, transformative period in their lives, and it's an honour to be a part of their journey.

Fostering Engagement and Positive Behaviour

If you are anything like me, you'll find that one of the biggest challenges of running a Beaver meeting is the "crowd control" element. Beavers are full of energy, they have many questions and their social awareness is not yet fully developed. When I started out, I often found myself with various problems of managing the group.

- Getting sidetracked into a conversation with one Beaver when I am trying to start an activity for the group.
- One Beaver is not interested in the activity and wanders off to do something else that then distracts the other children.
- A small group of high energy boys (it's usually boys!) start wrestling or having a rough game of tag when we are trying to do an activity.
- One Beaver gets upset and draws the attention of the scouter away from the activity.

Emily Battle is a primary school teacher and our Beaver leader at 175th Castleknock. She has a way with the kids that is incredible to behold. She can take a group of 24 rowdy, excited 6–8-year-olds running around a hall and, within less than a minute, turn them into a quiet circle of well-behaved Beaver Scouts ready to take instruction or do an activity.

I used the fact that I'm writing this book an excuse to get Emily to write down and share her tops tips for managing the group, here they are:

Create physical spaces: Establish designated areas, like a circle or line on the floor, to help Beavers understand where to gather or queue.

Capture full attention: Before addressing the group, ensure that you have everyone's undivided attention. A lot of groups use a quiet hand signal that spreads through the crowd when they see each other stop moving and put their hand up in the air.

Engage through counting: Count down/up to a number. This gives the Beavers a chance to finish their conversations or kick the ball away and settle into paying attention. As a nice twist, you can add a competitive element, for example, "last time you were all ready when I counted to 15. Can you get ready quicker this time?". Or, "Can you get ready before I count to zero?"

Interactive directions: Direct them to interact with their surroundings, asking them to point to various parts of the room like the ceiling, floor, or a particular object. This is a bit like a game that can start immediately and get everyone involved quickly.

Encourage rhythm: Clapping games or rhythmic activities can engage Beavers and help them to focus. Teach them to copy the series of claps that you do as a sort of echo.

Call and response: Create memorable phrases to bring the group's attention back to you.

Call - "1, 2, 3, eyes on me"

Response – "1, 2, eyes on you"

Or

Call "Macaroni and cheese"

Response "Everybody freeze"

Reward exemplary behaviour: Highlight and praise Beavers exhibiting desirable behaviour. This not only encourages that individual, but also sets an example for others.

""I'm going to ask Emily because she has her hand up and is sitting quietly".

"Emily is ready. Eunice is ready.....etc."

Incentives: Consider unique rewards, such as allowing the best-behaved Beaver to wear a special neckerchief or be the line leader for the next activity.

Quiet Corner: Having a special "quiet corner" for reflection or calming down can be beneficial. Simply telling the kids that it is there and offering for them to come over and sit in the quiet corner for a few minutes can incentivise rowdy kids to get back involved in the activity or give them a place to speak to one of the other scouters 1:1

Allocate a roving Scouter: Having a scouter who is not involved in the activity being vigilant and ready to engage with a wandering Beaver can be a great help to the person who is running the task. This is a great job for a new scouter who is learning the ropes.

Use the Small Groups System: Scouting has developed and refined it's framework over many years and it works really well! The principle of "small group system" – breaking the Beavers into lodges of 4-6 children for activities is a brilliant way to allow focus on more complicated activities.

Managing the Meeting

Emily also shared with me her top tips on managing the meeting. This is a bit of a checklist that she mentally runs through each week before and throughout the meeting to help make sure everyone is safe and that the admin of scouting is easy.

Uphold the correct ratios: Consistently maintain appropriate Beaver to leader ratios for all activities, whether they're indoors, outdoors, or overnight.

Section	Age Range	Youth Members	Scouters
Beaver Scouts	6-8	4-16	3
		Each Additional 4	1
Cub Scouts	9-11	4-16	3
		Each Additional 6	1
Scouts	12-15	4-16	2
		Each Additional 8	1
Venture Scouts	16-18	4-16	2
		Each Additional 16	1
Rover Scouts	18+	Any Number	0

(I've included the ratios for the other sections as I can never find them when I need them! – Please note, there are different ratios of you are travelling abroad with the children)

Document attendance: Record the presence of every Beaver at the start, adding any latecomers to maintain an accurate count. This is going to be useful for figuring out who achieved which badges, and also spotting when a Beaver stops coming and you might need to have a chat with their parents.

Regularly count Beavers: Perform a 'head-count' when regrouping, e.g. if you are returning to the hall from outside, or moving from one location to another during an excursion.

Buddy system: Get the kids to "buddy-up" in twos or threes and ask them to look out for each other.

Use routine: A consistent start and end to every meeting provides a sense of predictability and security for the Beavers. We like to have a game running while everyone is arriving, then kick off with an explanation of the plan for the evening and finish with the Beaver Shout (1,2,3 – who are we...).

Curbing wandering: Appoint a leader to gently guide any stray Beavers back to their designated areas, ensuring minimal disruption to the group's activity.

Safe dismissal: Reinforce the rule that Beavers must wait to be individually dismissed by a leader, who will then hand them over to their parent or guardian.

Preparing for outings: Prior to any outdoor excursions, reiterate safety rules

- Buddy system
- Always have a leader at the start and end of the line
- Child Protection – never be in a group of 2 – minimum size is 3 people

Using the toilet: Beavers should ask a Scouter for permission to leave the hall to use the toilet and check in with that Scouter when they are back. Ideally, a Scouter will stand at the hall door, with the toilet door in view, until the Beaver returns.

Be vigilant with food allergies: Especially on evenings involving food, check all ingredients for potential allergens and remind parents to keep you informed about any dietary restrictions their child might have.

Photography consent: Always respect the privacy of Beavers and their families. Ensure you have proper consent before taking or using any photographs and share this information with all leaders.

Roles

We've found over the years that these approaches work/ They are a great way of making sure the meetings go well. There are also a few roles that you can dish out among your leaders to make sure that all the work doesn't fall on just one or two people. Have a chat with your leaders and figure out who is going to take these roles and who will cover for them when they are not able to be there:

Roles	Responsibility / Deputy
Activity lead (changes each week – usually 2 people)	
Camps, Hikes and Outings	
Uniform Co-Ordinator	
Roll Call / Badges	
Pictures, Social Media & Parental comms	
Games Leader	
First Aider	

Planning
We also get together before every term starts on a zoom call or in the pub to plan out the activities for the next few months. We put the big things (camps, hikes and excursions) in the diary well in advance so there is plenty of time to plan for them. These calls give the whole term structure and give everyone a chance to influence and get involved with planning and activities.

For the calls, I like to bring along a lot of ideas from books like "the Scouting Trail" and Scouting Irelands "Adventure Skills" you can even use chat GPT to create lots of ideas. Hopefully you'll all have a copy of The Brilliant Beaver Guidebook as well to us for these planning meetings 😊.

Keeping a log
It's nice for the kids to have a record of their own achievements, you can buy a little notebook to give to each of them, or you can use the accompanying "Brilliant Beaver Logbook" that is available from all good scout shops and online.

I'd recommend that you keep these in your den or hall and update them as part of the meeting. Only let the kids take them home when they move on to cubs – otherwise you'll never see them again and an opportunity to create a nice memento of their Beaver days will have gone missing.

Planning for Fun: The Principles of Great Activities

Crafting activities for Beaver Scouts is a fascinating challenge. It's about creating an environment where fun meets learning, where energy meets creativity, and where every Beaver feels engaged and included. These are some principles that I've found useful to guide us in designing really positive experiences for our Beavers.

Working in Lodges

First and foremost, consider the power of the small group or 'Lodge.' Lodges allow Beavers to interact closely, foster a sense of camaraderie, and take responsibility as a team. It also makes managing activities easier for us as leaders. The purpose is not just to complete the activity but to enable the Beavers to learn, grow, and have fun together. We often select a lodge leader for our lodges, but unlike in the older sections, we tend to move it around so everyone gets a chance to be the leader. Older kids can understand that if they wait a couple of years, they will have a chance to be a Sixer or a Patrol Leader, but for Beavers, the world exists in much shorter timescales. If a 6-year-old is upset about not being lodge leader this week, it's much easier to explain that they will get a chance to lead next week rather than in 2-years.

Burning off Energy

Beavers are bundles of energy waiting to explode. Incorporating games and physical activities into your plan helps them channel this energy positively. Whether it's a high-energy game of tag, a nature scavenger hunt, or a team-building challenge, these activities keep them active and engaged while promoting healthy physical development.

Incorporating SPICES

An effective activity engages not just the body, but also the mind and spirit. This is where the concept of SPICES comes into play. SPICES stands for

- Social
- Physical
- Intellectual
- Character
- Emotional
- Spiritual

development. By incorporating these elements into our activities, we ensure a holistic development approach.

For instance, a group art project might engage them physically (painting, crafts), intellectually (planning the design), socially (working as a team), and emotionally (expressing themselves through art). Every activity can be a multi-faceted learning experience.

The role of religion in Scouting has changed significantly over the years. Some groups retain a religious element, others focus more on mindfulness and reflection for the spiritual element of the SPICES. This can be a controversial topic, so have a chat with your fellow Scouters and find out what the tradition and ethos of your group is, and help to support and develop that.

Plan, Do, Review

The Scouting approach to learning is encapsulated in the 'Plan, Do, Review' cycle. This process encourages Beavers to take ownership of their activities, reflect on their experiences, and learn from them.

Involving Beavers in planning helps them feel invested in the activity. Encourage them to brainstorm ideas, make decisions, and prepare for the task. After the activity, you can facilitate a short review session where they can share their experiences, discuss what they learned, and suggest improvements. This process not only enhances their learning but also develops their decision-making and problem-solving skills.

Time it Right

When it comes to activity duration, less is often more for Beavers. A typical 6 to 8-year-old has an attention span of about 15 to 20 minutes for a single activity. However, this can vary based on the nature of the activity, the time of day, and the individual child. It's essential to keep activities varied and dynamic to hold their interest.

Reading the Room

As leaders, it's crucial to stay attuned to the Beavers' energy levels and engagement. Are they excited and involved, or are they losing interest? Are they tired, or can they handle another activity? Reading the room will help you adjust your plans on the go and maintain a positive and enjoyable environment.

The ultimate goal is to create an atmosphere where the Beavers feel safe, valued, and excited to learn and grow. With thoughtful planning and a good understanding of our Beavers, we can design activities that they'll look back on with a big smile. Let the fun begin!

Theme Nights: Making Regular Meetings Extraordinary

Theme nights can turn ordinary Beaver meetings into extraordinary adventures. They add an element of excitement and novelty, capturing the Beavers' imagination and enthusiasm. But how can we make these theme nights truly unforgettable? The answer lies in the power of storytelling.

The Role of Storytelling in Scouting

Storytelling has always been an integral part of Scouting. It's a tool that helps us connect with the Beavers, engage their imagination, and make learning fun and meaningful. A well-told story can transport Beavers into different worlds, help them see from different perspectives, and inspire them to dream and explore.

For Beaver Scouts, stories provide a symbolic framework through which they can understand and interact with the world. They can see themselves as brave adventurers, clever problem-solvers, or caring friends, embodying the principles of the Scout Law in their imagined adventures.

Crafting Theme Nights with Stories

So how can we incorporate storytelling into our theme nights? Here are a few ideas:

Start with a Story: Kick off your theme night with a captivating story that sets the stage for the evening. It could be a tale of pirates searching for a hidden treasure, astronauts exploring a new planet, or superheroes saving the day. This story gives context to the activities and sparks the Beavers' imagination right from the start.

Create a Storyline: Instead of isolated activities, consider creating a storyline that connects all the activities of the evening. Each activity becomes a chapter in your adventure, keeping the Beavers engaged and invested throughout.

Involve the Beavers in the Story: Make the Beavers active participants in your story. They could be detectives solving a mystery, explorers overcoming obstacles, or inventors creating a revolutionary gadget. When they're part of the story, the learning becomes personal and impactful.

Use Props and Costumes: Props and costumes can add a touch of magic to your theme night. They can transform your meeting place into a pirate ship, a jungle, or a spaceship and make your story come alive. Plus, they're a lot of fun!

End with a Reflection: Conclude your theme night with a reflection on the story. What did the Beavers learn from their adventure? How did they embody the Scout Promise and Law in their story? This reflection helps them connect their imagined experiences with real-life principles and lessons.

I have always found that coming up with ideas when planning for nights can be tough. This book is about helping you to become a Brilliant Beaver leader, so I have collated a list of ideas that you can use. Please feel free to tweak and change these as you see fit.

Suggested Themes for Beaver Activities

Pirate Adventure: Beavers turn into pirates, seeking hidden treasure. Activities can include a treasure hunt, map-making, and pirate-themed crafts. Use words like 'Ahoy,' 'treasure,' and 'adventure.'

Wild West: Beavers are cowboys and cowgirls in the Old West. Try a lasso challenge, learning about animals of the West, or making bandanas. Use words like 'howdy,' 'yeehaw,' and 'roundup.'

Under the Sea: Dive into an ocean adventure. Activities can involve learning about sea creatures, making fish crafts, or singing sea shanties. Introduce characters like a wise old turtle or a playful dolphin.

Rainforest Expedition: Beavers are explorers in a lush rainforest. Plan nature walks, animal spotting, or planting seeds. Use words like 'discovery,' 'nature,' and 'adventure.'

Space Explorers: Beavers are astronauts exploring the cosmos. Try stargazing, rocket-building, or learning about planets. Introduce characters like friendly aliens or wise, old stars.

Castle and Knights: Transform into knights and princesses in a medieval castle. Try a 'dragon egg' hunt, a castle-building competition, or a knight's obstacle course.

Around the World: Beavers 'travel' to different countries. Activities can include food tasting, learning basic foreign words, or crafting national flags. Use words like 'journey,' 'explore,' and 'culture.'

Dinosaur Dig: Beavers become palaeontologists discovering dinosaurs. Plan a mock fossil dig, dinosaur crafts, or learning about different dinosaurs. Introduce characters like a friendly T-Rex or a clever Velociraptor.

Magical Creatures: Enter a world of unicorns, dragons, and fairies. Activities can include storytelling, magic tricks, or creating fairy gardens. Use words like 'magic,' 'wonder,' and 'imagination.'

Garden Growers: Beavers become gardeners. Activities can involve planting seeds, learning about insects, or making bird feeders. Use words like 'grow,' 'nature,' and 'nurture.'

Spy Academy: Train to be top secret agents. Plan a code-breaking challenge, a stealth obstacle course, or learning about real-life spies. Use words like 'secret,' 'mission,' and 'decode.'

Time Travellers: Beavers journey to different periods. Try crafting timelines, learning about historical figures, or recreating historical events. Use words like 'past,' 'future,' and 'discover.'

Super Sleuths: Beavers are detectives solving a mystery. Plan a whodunit game, fingerprinting activity, or clue finding. Use words like 'clue,' 'mystery,' and 'solve.'

Superhero Squad: Each Beaver becomes a superhero. Activities can include creating superhero badges, obstacle courses, or learning about real-life heroes. Use words like 'power,' 'hero,' and 'rescue.'

Artists' Studio: Beavers become artists for the day. Activities can include painting, sculpture-making, or learning about famous artists. Use words like 'create,' 'imagine,' and 'masterpiece.'

Insect Inspectors: Beavers turn into entomologists studying insects. Plan an insect hunt, insect drawing, or learning about the life cycle of a butterfly. Use words like 'discover,' 'nature,' and 'investigate.'

Circus Fun: Step into the fun world of the circus. Try juggling, clowning around, or making circus-themed crafts. Use words like 'spectacle,' 'entertain,' and 'perform.'

Fairy Tales: Dive into the world of classic fairy tales. Activities can include acting out stories, puppet-making, or creating their fairy tales. Use words like 'once upon a time,' 'magic,' and 'adventure.'

Sports Day: Organize a day of various sports. Plan mini games, learn about sportsmanship, or create team banners. Use words like 'teamwork,' 'challenge,' and 'victory.'

Farm Life: Beavers learn about life on a farm. Activities can include a virtual farm visit, learning about different farm animals, or making butter. Use words like 'harvest,' 'care,' and 'grow.' We recently had a visit from a lamb, and a couple of chicks to one of our Beaver meetings – Thanks Al!

Arctic Explorers: Beavers turn into explorers in the Arctic. Try building 'igloos' with marshmallows, learning about polar animals, or making snow-themed crafts. Use words like 'explore,' 'cold,' and 'survive.'

Island Survival: Beavers are stranded on a desert island. Plan a shelter-building activity, learn about edible plants, or create a message in a bottle. Use words like 'survive,' 'resourceful,' and 'teamwork.'

Polar Express: Beavers board the Polar Express for a Christmas adventure. Try making Christmas decorations, singing carols, or storytelling. Use words like 'believe,' 'gift,' and 'journey.'

Heroes of History: Beavers learn about historical figures. Plan role-playing games, timeline crafts, or a 'guess who' game. Use words like 'inspire,' 'history,' and 'change.'

Mad Scientists: Beavers are scientists making exciting discoveries. Try simple experiments, learning about famous scientists, or making lab coats. Use words like 'invent,' 'discover,' and 'experiment.'

Mountain Climbers: Beavers turn into mountaineers. Try a climbing wall activity, learn about mountain animals, or make mountain art. Use words like 'climb,' 'peak,' and 'challenge.'

Back to Nature: Beavers connect with nature. Plan a nature scavenger hunt, leaf-rubbing activity, or learn about different trees. Use words like 'explore,' 'discover,' and 'nature.'

Dessert Chefs: Beavers become bakers for the day. Try a simple baking activity, decorating cupcakes, or learning about healthy eating. Use words like 'bake,' 'create,' and 'delicious.'

World of Music: Dive into different music styles. Activities can include making simple instruments, learning about different music genres, or a dance-off. Use words like 'rhythm,' 'melody,' and 'perform.'

Jungle Journey: Venture into the wild jungle. Activities can include animal yoga, making animal masks, or learning about jungle ecosystems. Use words like 'wild,' 'explore,' and 'adventure.'

Theme nights are great, and they don't have to be complicated, a simple short story at the start of the night can set the scene for some amazing activities.

Theme nights are an opportunity to step out of the ordinary and dive into a world of imagination and excitement. With storytelling at the helm, we can create memorable experiences that not only entertain our Beavers but also inspire them to learn, grow, and dream.

Stories and fun

My auntie Janet suggested that we include one of her favourite activities in this book. The concept is to use an immersive story for a game. In this game, each Beaver Scout is assigned a role, that of a specific animal - a fox, a badger, a mole, a mouse, or an owl. As the leader reads the story, whenever the animal character corresponding to a Beaver's role is mentioned, that Beaver jumps up and runs around the circle. Initially, the roles are mentioned with generous intervals in between, allowing each Beaver a chance to respond and partake in the fun. As the story progresses, the animal characters are mentioned more frequently, resulting in more Beavers running around, adding to the excitement and energy of the story. It's up to you to pace the story to maximise the fun and silliness, while making sure you don't lose too much structure.

Here's the story – you can, of course, make your own ones up as well based on the themes above.

The Storm

Once upon a time, in a vast and serene forest, there lived five animals who had never met. The ***fox*** lived by the whispering stream, the ***badger*** dwelled under the towering trees, the ***mole*** nested deep underground, the ***mouse*** made home amidst the lush ferns, and the ***owl*** perched in a mighty oak.

One sunny day, the ***fox*** decided to venture out of his comfort zone. As he trotted along, he met the ***badger***, who was out looking for food. The ***fox*** and the ***badger*** exchanged friendly greetings, marking the start of a new friendship.

Deep underground, the ***mole*** sensed the vibrations of their conversation and decided to investigate. Popping out of his hole, he was surprised to see the *fox* and the ***badger***. Joining their friendly chatter, he was welcomed warmly by the duo.

The friendly banter and laughter echoed across the forest and reached the small, curious ***mouse***. Encouraged by their cheerful sounds, he timidly approached the ***mole***. He was greeted with a smile, making her feel instantly welcome.

Watching everything from the tall oak tree was the ***owl***. He was intrigued by the camaraderie developing on the ground. He swooped down and hooted a warm hello to the *others*.

As they chatted away, sharing stories and experiences, the owl noticed the sky turning a dark, ominous grey. A storm was brewing. The ***badger*** suggested they needed to seek shelter.

Suddenly, the heavens opened, and it started to pour. The stream beside which the *fox* lived started to swell rapidly. Realizing the impending danger, the ***mouse*** alerted the *owl* who flew up into the sky to , find higher ground to escape the flood.

The *fox* swiftly led the way with the ***badger, mole and mouse,*** close behind her. The journey was fraught with challenges, but their collective efforts and courage kept them going. The ***mouse***, being the smallest, struggled to keep up, but the ***badger***, helped him along.

Finally, they reached a safe, dry spot, where they huddled together, their spirits high despite the situation. Their adventure had solidified their bond, and they found comfort in their newfound friendship.

As the storm passed, and the water levels started to recede. The *fox*, ***badger***, ***mole***, ***mouse***, and *owl* returned to their homes, promising to stay connected and help each other in times of need.

And so, they *all* lived happily ever after.

The Great Outdoors: Planning Day Trips and Weekend Excursions

One of the fundamental pillars of Scouting is the appreciation and understanding of the great outdoors. There's a world of adventure waiting just outside our doorstep, full of opportunities for learning, exploration, and fun. In this chapter, we'll dive into the benefits and logistics of planning day trips and weekend excursions for your Beaver Scouts.

There's something incredibly fulfilling about stepping out of the familiar surroundings of the den or sports hall and immersing ourselves in the natural world. It's a chance to break the routine, stimulate the senses, and instil a sense of adventure in our young Beavers. Not to mention, it provides an excellent opportunity to engage with our local community, visit places of interest, and learn about our environment first-hand.

We are very lucky in our group to have lots of different leaders, with a wide range of skills. Some of the Scouters, like Emily and Eunice have an incredible way of interacting with the kids that calms them and makes the activities possible. Others like Jim and Al bring special skills or interests like backwoods and farming. One of the Scouters, Bernard who joined us last year seems to know absolutely everybody in the village. Within just a few of months of joining, Bernard had organised a visit from a firefighter, a nature trip hosted by an inspiring expert from the Office of Public Works and a barge trip on the canal. Using your skills and connections is part of being a Beaver leader, so, even if you are a brand-new Beaver leader, if you think of an idea, just run with it. As long as it's safe, the other Scouters and the kids will be delighted that you have taken responsibility and made something happen.

Outdoor excursions don't just offer a change of scenery. They're an opportunity to instil values such as respect for nature, teamwork, and responsibility. They teach Beavers to be adaptable, curious, and resilient. And, of course, these outings also allow Beavers to burn off some energy and keep active, which is crucial for their physical health and well-being.

When planning these trips, consider the myriad of destinations at your disposal. There's so much more to explore beyond the conventional field trips. From local farms and nature reserves to museums and historical sites, each place holds a unique educational experience for our Beavers. And while these trips can sometimes require more planning and preparation than regular meetings, the rewards are immeasurable.

Involving the community in your trips can also yield wonderful results. Perhaps a local baker could show your Beavers how bread is made, or a park ranger could give them a guided tour of a nature reserve. This not only helps Beavers understand their community better but also strengthens the ties between your Scout group and the community.

Your group of leaders you may already know many of the people who can help you to organise these kinds of activities. But don't underestimate the power of the neckerchief. Most people are delighted to be able to help the Scouts, simply emailing local organisations or turning up in a neckerchief and asking to speak to someone about organising activities can provide many opportunities for these kinds of activities.

Here are some ideas to get your creative juices flowing when it comes to planning trips and activities:

Caving Experience: Explore local caves and learn about geological formations. Experienced caving guides can ensure safety and provide interesting facts about the cave systems.

Fire Station Visit: Learn about fire safety and the roles of firefighters. The local fire department may be able to arrange a visit.

Rock Climbing: A great activity to promote physical fitness and problem-solving. Climbing instructors can provide safety instructions and guidance either indoor or outdoor.

Canoeing Adventure: Develop teamwork and paddling skills. Certified canoeing instructors can provide the necessary training and guidance.

Outdoor Survival Skills Workshop: Learn about building shelter, finding food, and navigation. Survival experts can conduct this hands-on workshop.

Ziplining Adventure: Experience the thrill of ziplining. Certified instructors can ensure safety and provide the necessary guidance.

Horseback Riding Experience: Learn basic horse riding skills and animal care. Local stables or equestrian centers can provide trained horses and riding instructors.

Sailing Trip: Learn about sailing and water safety. Local sailing clubs or schools can provide a hands-on sailing experience.

Mountain Biking Excursion: Enjoy local trails while promoting physical fitness. Local cycling clubs can provide mountain biking instruction and ensure safety.

High Ropes Course: Develop balance, coordination and confidence. Certified instructors can provide safety briefing and guidance.

Outdoor First Aid Course: Learn important life-saving skills. First aid trainers can provide this practical workshop.

Local Park Exploration: Organize scavenger hunts, birdwatching or tree identification activities. Get assistance from park rangers or local naturalists.

Beach Trip: If you're near the coast, a beach day could include sandcastle building, beach clean-up or a marine life study. Reach out to marine biologists or conservation groups.

Birdhouse Building Workshop: Develop practical skills and promote love for nature. A craftsman or nature conservationist can guide the activity.

Kayaking Excursion: Learn basic paddling skills and enjoy local water bodies. Certified kayaking instructors can provide a safety briefing and basic kayaking lesson.

Community Garden Visit: Learn about different plants, composting and gardening techniques. Gardeners or horticulturists could give a guided tour or workshop.

Walking Tour of Your Town: Explore local landmarks and learn about the town's history. A local historian or tour guide could lead this activity.

Visit a Farm: Understand where food comes from and how a farm works. The farm owner or workers can provide a tour and answer questions.

Recycling Centre Tour: Understand the importance of recycling and how the process works. Reach out to the local recycling centre for tour possibilities.

Geocaching Adventure: Promote problem-solving, teamwork, and enjoy the outdoors. Outdoor enthusiasts or geocaching clubs could guide this activity.

Visit a Local News Station: Learn about broadcasting and news production. The station's staff might give a tour and explain their work.

Participate in a Festival or Event: Understand culture and traditions. Event organizers or community leaders can explain the significance of the event.

Visit a Wind or Solar Farm: Understand renewable energy sources and their importance. Energy company representatives can provide a tour or demonstration.

Hiking a Local Trail: Discover local wildlife and develop physical fitness. Local outdoor or hiking clubs could help plan the hike and ensure safety.

Library Visit: Promote a love for reading and learning. A librarian can organize a story time or library tour.

Nature Reserve Visit: Learn about local ecosystems and conservation efforts. Park rangers or conservationists can provide guided tours or workshops.

Visit a Local Market: Understand local produce, crafts and trades. Market vendors could talk about their products or skills.

Local Sports Match: Promote teamwork and sportsmanship. Athletes or coaches can talk about the importance of fitness and fair play.

Local Craft Workshop: Develop creativity and motor skills. Artisans or craft teachers can conduct a simple craft workshop.

Visit a Historical Site: Learn about local history and heritage. Museum staff or historians could provide a tour or talk.

Observatory Visit: Understand stars, planets and space. Astronomers or observatory staff can provide a tour or star-gazing session.

Visit an Animal Shelter: Promote empathy and care for animals. Shelter staff can talk about their work and how to care for pets.

Wildlife Spotting Excursion: Identify local wildlife and learn about their habitats. Wildlife experts or birdwatchers can guide the activity.

Orienteering Course: Improve map-reading and navigation skills in a local park. Orienteering clubs can set up courses and provide instructions.

Cycling Excursion: Promote physical fitness and explore local surroundings. Local cycling clubs could help plan the route and ensure safety.

Archery Lesson: Develop focus and hand-eye coordination. Certified archery instructors can provide the necessary training and guidance.

Visit to a Senior Citizen Home: Promote empathy, respect and inter-generational understanding. The care home staff can coordinate the visit.

Visit a Factory or Bakery: Understand how things are made. Factory or bakery staff can provide a tour or demonstration.

Local River or Lake Visit: Learn about freshwater ecosystems. Conservationists or naturalists can provide a guided tour or workshop.

Visit to a Garda Station: Understand the role of the police in the community. The Garda community support team can help

Botanical Garden Visit: Learn about various plant species and their importance. Botanists or garden staff can provide a tour or workshop.

Tree Planting Activity: Understand the importance of trees and promote environmental stewardship. Environmental groups can help plan the activity.

Community Clean-Up: Promote environmental stewardship and community service. Environmental or community groups can organize the activity.

As you continue your journey as a Beaver Leader, keep in mind that each day trip or weekend excursion you plan is another opportunity to create lasting memories, spark curiosity, and foster a love for the great outdoors in your Beavers.

Taming the Wild: Camping for Beaver Leaders

Running great evening meetings and community activities is amazing and powerful, but if you are not camping, you are not really Scouting. You might have 30-40 hour-long meetings throughout the year with your Beavers. If you manage to go on a couple of overnight adventures and a weekend camp during the year, that 30-40 hours becomes more like 100 – excluding sleep!

Camping brings the group together, it gives you a chance to do longer activities under less time pressure, and it is among the most exciting things that Beavers can do. The buzz and energy that you get that first night on Summer camp is one of the best feelings in Scouting.

It's a special kind of magic that happens when we trade in our usual surroundings for the rustling trees, crackling campfire, and starlit skies. But, as enchanting as it may sound, it requires careful planning and preparation to ensure a safe, enjoyable, and memorable experience for our Beavers.

To guide you through this process, I've summarised Scouting Irelands "Camping with the stars" booklet here. It's a brilliant resource that presents a step-by-step approach to organising a camp for Beavers or Cubs.

Step 1: First Pitch - Planning is vital for a successful camp. Start by dividing your Beavers into small groups or Lodges, each with their assigned Scouter. Discuss roles and responsibilities, and involve the Beavers in the planning process to build anticipation and ownership.

Step 2: Gearing Up - Every camper needs the right gear. Talk about the importance of proper clothing and layering, packing a personal first aid kit, and maintaining hygiene while camping. Discuss how to pack an overnight bag efficiently.

Kit list for camping

- ☐ NECKERCHIEF (must be worn at all times)
- ☐ Full uniform (worn travelling to and from the camp)
- ☐ Sleeping bag
- ☐ Ground mat
- ☐ Hiking boots
- ☐ Trainers or comfortable shoes
- ☐ 3-5 changes of clothes (depending on length of camp)
- ☐ Fleece/hoody/warm jumper
- ☐ Underwear
- ☐ Several pairs of socks
- ☐ Waterproof trousers and jacket
- ☐ Sleep wear (warm pyjamas or track suit)
- ☐ Hand towel
- ☐ Wash bag
- ☐ Mug, plate, bowl, knife, fork, spoon
- ☐ Drinks bottle
- ☐ Plastic bags (for keeping wet clothes / boots separate)
- ☐ Day bag or small rucksack
- ☐ Pillow (or pillowcase to stuff with clothes)
- ☐ Torch (and extra batteries)
- ☐ Toothbrush, Toothpaste, Soap & container, Shampoo
- ☐ Washcloth
- ☐ Comb/hairbrush
- ☐ Small hand towel
- ☐ Camp mascot (teddy bear)
- ☐ IF HOT - sun protection (sun cream and a hat)
- ☐ IF COLD – gloves, hat

Step 3: Out and About - Plan a day activity that requires the Beavers to use their gear. This could be a hike or a nature trail, focusing on the importance of carrying the right equipment for the day's adventure.

Step 4: Site and Oversight - Teach your Beavers about the Leave No Trace principles, risk management, and how to choose and set up a campsite. This is a great opportunity to impart respect for nature and the importance of safety.

Step 5: Food for Thought - Plan an overnight trip that includes food preparation and hygiene. Beavers can learn how to cook simple meals in small groups, reinforcing teamwork and essential survival skills.

Step 6: Spars and Sparks - Introduce your Beavers to the basics of tent pitching, constructing camp gadgets, and fire-lighting. These practical skills are essential for any camper and also help to foster a sense of accomplishment.

Step 7: Adding the Magic - Camping is more than just survival skills; it's about creating memorable experiences. Organize a campfire, a Scouts' Own reflective session, a flag ceremony, a gear check, and a revision of what they've learned. These traditions are the soul of Scouting and make camping truly special.

Step 8: Camping with the Stars - Finally, it's time to put all the planning and preparation into action. Go out, camp, and have fun! Afterwards, review the experience with your Beavers to learn from it and plan for future adventures.

Check out "Camping with the Stars" for a much more detailed guidance on these areas.

Backwoods for Beavers

One of the main reasons a lot of people get involved in scouting is to get outside and into nature. The ability to survive in the wilderness is one of my favourite things to learn about, but it can be difficult to have confidence around Beavers when you are talking about knives, axes and fire. Jim O'Carroll joined our beaver group a couple of years ago and has given us a new appreciation for all things backwoods. It now forms a big part of what we do, and the evenings he runs are amongst the most popular ones of the year.

Safety is crucial when you are getting involved in these kinds of activities, and while it is great to see scouts whittling sculptures and chopping up logs, you need to be quite careful with younger children. I've found that most things tried out safely when have enough adults to teach 1:1 with Beavers, but as soon as you add crowd control into the mix it becomes too hard to focus on activities that are inherently risky. That's why the activities in this chapter are designed to be relatively safe, while giving the children a taste of what is coming later in their scouting careers.

That said, it is your responsibility as an adult scouter to make sure you don't try to undertake anything that is too risky. You know the children and the equipment you are using best, so be safe, and don't take any risks with these kinds of activities. It is possible to hurt yourself while gathering firewood, cutting yourself on a potato peeler and climbing into a hammock, so try to keep these activities relatively low energy and take a break for a game if the children start to get too restless.

But you can also have a lot of fun with these activities. They designed not only to teach but to engage and entertain. The sense of achievement the Beavers feel after completing each task is truly invaluable, so I would encourage you to try and weave some of these into your programmes over the Summer months whenever possible.

One scouting principle that is worth keeping at the forefront of your mind with these is to 'Leave No Trace'. Being active in nature requires a respect that ensures we leave the environment in as good a state or better than we found it. Talk about this with the children and encourage them to point out any rubbish they see to be picked up safely (watch out for broken glass!)

Jim and I enjoyed a very pleasant evening writing up these activities, we hope that you will enjoy them as much as we do!

Firewood Collection

Objective: Teach children how to identify and collect suitable firewood.

Equipment: Gloves, sacks or baskets for collecting

Method: Guide the beavers in identifying deadwood off the ground, which is best for burning. Teach them to look for twigs that snap easily and do not have any green inside, indicating they are dry and will burn well. Divide the group into pairs and give them each a sack or basket for collecting wood. This activity is best done in a wooded area where there are plenty of fallen branches. The kids could then "grade" the wood they have collected by sorting it into tinder (pencil lead thickness), kindling (pencil thickness), small sticks (thumb thickness), Large sticks (wrist thickness and bigger).

Making Firelighters with Egg Boxes and Wax

Objective: Learn to create homemade firelighters.

Equipment: Egg carton, candle wax, sawdust or cotton balls and an old pot.

Method: Melt the wax in the old pot. Fill each egg carton section with sawdust of cotton wool and pour melted wax over it until it's soaked. Allow to cool and harden. The Beavers can then break off a section to start a fire. This activity should be done under close adult supervision indoors or outdoors with a controlled fire setup. Leave a bit of the cotton wool or a few very small stick "sticking out" of each section to provide a "wick" to light.

Starting a Fire

Objective: Learn how to start a fire using flint and steel.

Equipment: Flint & steel (ferro rod), cotton wool, petroleum jelly.

Method: Show the beavers how to coat a piece of cotton wool with petroleum jelly. Then demonstrate striking the fire rod to create a spark, directing it towards the coated cotton wool to ignite it. This activity should be done under close adult supervision, and outdoors in a fire-safe area.

Water Purification

Objective: Understand the principles of water purification.

Equipment: Clear plastic bottle with the bottom cut off, charcoal, cotton, pebbles, sand, dirty water (for demonstration), pot for boiling water, fire source.

Method: Show the beavers how to layer charcoal, sand, pebbles, and cotton in the bottle with the finest mesh at the bottom, then pour dirty water through it. Explain this is the first step of filtration, but the water is not yet safe to drink. Boil the filtered water to ensure it's safe for consumption and add a water purification tablet or iodine as an extra talking point / safety feature. Always under adult supervision.

Note: Jim did this activity with the Beavers at our last Summer camp, and the t-shirt he used had been recently washed in detergent. The bubbles appeared in the water and made it taste really bad!! Maybe use a t-shirt that has been through a couple of rinse cycles first.

One Match Fire

Objective: Learn how to efficiently start a fire using only one match.

Equipment: Match, tinder, kindling, firewood.

Method: Explain to the beavers the importance of preparation when starting a fire. Teach them how to create a fire lay with tinder, kindling, and firewood. Then, they should strike the match and use it to ignite the tinder. The challenge for the Beavers is in preparing the fire so well that it will start with only one match. You can talk about the risks of needing to shield your match from the wind and re-enforce the importance of dry materials set up correctly.

Setting Up a Hammock

Objective: Learn how to set up a hammock and sleep in it safely.

Equipment: Hammock, suitable trees or hammock stands.

Method: Show the beavers how to properly attach a hammock to trees or a hammock stand. Discuss the best practices for safely getting in and out of the hammock to avoid falling. This can be done outdoors, ideally in a forested area. Set the hammocks up nice and low so that they can fall out safely. They will almost certainly want to swing in them, so make sure you tie the knots well. I like to use a double figure of eight.

Note: If you don't know a lot about knots – check out the "knots 3D" app – I use it all the time when I can't remember how to do one!

Bark Peeling with Vegetable Peelers

Objective: Learn how to safely remove bark from branches using vegetable peelers.

Equipment: Vegetable peelers, green branches.

Method: Demonstrate to the beavers how to safely use the peeler to remove bark from a branch. Supervise them as they practice this skill.

Edible Campfire

Objective: Create an edible campfire as a fun, creative activity.

Equipment: Biscuits, chocolate spread, candy floss, chocolate matchsticks, KitKat bars and mini marshmallows.

Method: The beavers create a miniature "campfire" by arranging biscuits as the fireplace, using chocolate spread for the dirt, candy floss as the tinder, chocolate matchsticks as the kindling, and KitKat bars as the logs. Place mini marshmallows around as the stone circle to prevent the fire from spreading. They will love this one, as they get to eat their fires afterwards!

Leaf Prints

Objective: Create prints using leaves and bark.

Equipment: Paper or cloth, crayons or chalk

Method: Have the beavers select interesting leaves and bark and create rubbings on paper or cloth with crayons or chalk. This activity is suitable for individual work but can also be a group project where each child contributes a few rubbings to create a collective artwork. Have a handy tree identification guidebook nearby so that you can confidently talk to the Beavers about the types of tree. You can even look them up in the guide together.

Starting a Fire Using Friction

Objective: Learn how to create a fire using an electric drill for friction.

Equipment: Electric drill, sharp knife, wooden dowel, piece of softwood, tinder.

Method: Demonstrate to the beavers how to create a small divot in the wood using the sharp knife next to a notch in the side of the softwood. Insert the dowel into the drill and place in the divot, then run the drill to generate friction. Once smoke appears and black dust gathers in the notch run the drill for a further 30 seconds to be sure you have created an ember. Transfer your ember to a bundle of tinder and blow gently to start a fire. This is done by and adult, but the kids can have a go on the drill if supervised carefully.

Shelter Building - Tree Forts

Objective: Learn how to create a basic natural shelter.

Equipment: None needed

Method: Guide Beavers to create simple, small shelters using fallen branches, leaves, and moss. Divide them into small groups of 3-4 and give each group a designated area for their shelter. This activity is best done in a forested area with plenty of loose natural materials. Don't worry too much about the weather proofing of the shelters, it's much more about having a fun activity and using your imagination. You could even play a wide game afterwards using the forts as bases.

Personal Progression - Using Adventure Skills to build an evening.

Personal progression is a vital aspect of the Scouting experience, particularly for Beaver Scouts who are at the beginning of their Scouting journey. It allows them to develop a wide range of skills, grow in confidence, and gain a deeper understanding of themselves and the world around them. Each Beaver Scout's progress is individual and unique, reflecting their own interests, abilities, and the pace at which they learn and develop.

Adventure Skills badges offer an excellent framework for personal progression. By working towards these badges, Beaver Scouts have the opportunity to learn practical skills, engage with their environment, and experience the thrill of discovery and achievement.

In this chapter, we will focus on Level 1 Adventure Skills for Beaver Scouts, providing examples of how you can build engaging, hands-on evening activities around these skills. The activities cover a wide range of areas -Camping, Backwoods, Hillwalking, Emergencies, Paddling, Sailing, Rowing, Pioneering, and Air Activities.

I've put together an example programme to develop each skill over two 1-hour sessions, with a strong focus on practical, hands-on experiences rather than just discussion. Beavers learn best when they're actively engaged in fun, challenging activities that allow them to put new skills into practice.

While I've been focused on Level 1 Adventure Skills, it's worth noting that the Beaver Scouts programme typically focuses on Levels 1 and 2. The activities suggested here for Level 1 could easily be adapted or extended for Level 2. I'd encourage readers to be creative and innovative in designing activities for their Beaver Scouts. The ideas presented here should be seen as a starting point, a source of inspiration that can be customized to suit the specific needs and interests of your group. I hope that they will spark your imagination and help you create a vibrant, exciting program that supports the personal progression of every Beaver Scout.

Adventure Skills – Camping stage 1

Session 1: Gear Up For Camping –
Objective: By the end of the session, Beavers will have a practical understanding of what personal gear is necessary for camping, how to pack their rucksack, and how to set up their sleeping area.

Equipment needed: Personal camping gear (sleeping bag, pillow, torch, toiletries, personal clothing), rucksack, tent and camping equipment.

Activity Plan:

1. Camping Gear Relay Race (15 minutes):
Set up a relay race where Beavers must run to a pile of camping gear, choose the correct items they would need for camping, and pack them into a rucksack. This will help them learn what gear is necessary and how to pack efficiently.

2. Sleeping Area Setup Workshop (20 minutes):
Provide each Beaver with a sleeping bag and a small space to set up their sleeping area. Discuss the importance of a good night's

sleep on camp and the best ways to arrange their sleeping area for comfort.

3. Gear Care Role Play (15 minutes):
Divide Beavers into pairs for a role-play activity. One Beaver will play the role of a 'camping expert' giving advice on how to care for camping gear, and the other will be a 'new camper' asking questions.

4. Clothes Sorting Game (10 minutes):
Have a variety of clothes for different weather conditions spread out. Ask Beavers to pick out what would be appropriate to wear for different weather scenarios.

Session 2: Pitching Tents and Emergency Preparedness

Objective: By the end of the session, Beavers will understand the basics of tent pitching, the importance of the Buddy System, and know the different emergency services available and when and how to contact them.

Equipment needed: Tent and camping equipment, small sticks, pictures or models of different emergency service vehicles, contact cards with emergency numbers.

Activity Plan:

1. Tent Pitching Workshop (20 minutes):
Demonstrate how to pitch a tent and allow the Beavers to practise in small groups. This hands-on experience will familiarize them with the process and the main parts of a tent.

2. Fire-Making Material Collection Race (10 minutes):
Hold a race where Beavers must search for small sticks suitable for fire-making (ensure this is done in a safe and supervised manner). This activity will teach them about sourcing fire-starting materials.

3. Buddy System Pairing Game (10 minutes):
Play a game where Beavers must find their 'buddy' by matching clues or symbols. This will reinforce the importance of the Buddy System in a fun, engaging way.

4. Emergency Services Quiz (10 minutes):
Use pictures or models of different emergency service vehicles for a quiz game. Ask Beavers to identify the service each vehicle belongs to, and discuss when and how to contact them.

5. Practice Emergency Call (10 minutes):
Role-play an emergency scenario where Beavers have to make a 'mock' emergency call. This will help them understand what information is important to give during such a call.

Adventure Skills – Backwoods stage 1

Session 1: Dressing for the Wilderness and Building Shelters
Objective: Beavers will learn what types of clothing are appropriate for wilderness excursions and gain hands-on experience in building a simple shelter.

Equipment Needed: Different types of clothing suitable for various weather conditions, natural materials for shelter building (sticks, leaves), and a tarpaulin or large sheet.

Activity Plan:

1. Clothing for Nature Relay Race (15 minutes):
Lay out a variety of clothing items suitable for different weather conditions. Divide Beavers into teams and have them race to dress a team member in appropriate clothing for a given scenario.

2. Shelter Building Workshop (30 minutes):
Demonstrate how to build a simple shelter using natural materials and a tarpaulin or large sheet. Divide Beavers into small groups and challenge them to construct their own shelters.

3. Reflection and Sharing (15 minutes):
Allow each group to present their shelter to the rest of the colony. Discuss what they did well and what they could improve next time.

Session 2: Fire Safety, Food Preparation, and Tool Use
Objective: Beavers will learn about fire safety, preparing food for cooking, and the safe use of hand tools. They will also understand what a basic survival kit should contain.

Equipment Needed: Fire-making equipment, food for preparation (such as vegetables and foil for making foil packet meals), hand tools (hammers, screwdrivers), and items for a basic survival kit.

Activity Plan:

1. Fire Safety Talk and Demonstration (15 minutes):
Discuss and demonstrate the safe way to behave around fires. Explain how to safely start and extinguish a fire.

2. Food Preparation Activity (15 minutes):
Have Beavers prepare vegetables for a foil packet meal. Discuss the importance of washing hands, cleaning food, and safe cutting techniques.

3. Safe Tool Use Demonstration and Practice (15 minutes):
Demonstrate the safe use of basic hand tools like an axe or a bow saw. Supervise Beavers as they practise using the tools on a safe task, such as sawing a log or chopping wood.

Note: Some people are uncomfortable with this kind of activity for Beavers, and you do have to be careful. We do this kind of thing quite often, but in very small groups, and we use 1:1 Supervision with an adult when they are actually handling the tools.

4. Survival Kit Assembly (15 minutes):
Show Beavers a basic survival kit and discuss what each item is for. Have Beavers put together a mock survival kit from a selection of items.

Adventure Skills – Pioneering stage 1

Session 1: Introduction to Pioneering and Equipment
Objective: Beavers will learn about the basics of pioneering, the equipment needed to make pioneering gadgets, and the importance of safety during pioneering activities.

Equipment Needed: Pioneering equipment (such as ropes, elastic bands, wooden poles), sample pioneering gadgets, emergency services contact list, safety guidelines.

Activity Plan:

1. Introduction to Pioneering (15 minutes):
Explain the basics of pioneering and show examples of simple pioneering gadgets. Discuss the importance of pioneering in Scouting.

2. Equipment Demonstration (20 minutes):
Show and explain the equipment needed for making pioneering gadgets. Let the Beavers handle the equipment under supervision to familiarize themselves with it.

3. Safety Discussion (10 minutes):

Discuss the importance of safety during pioneering activities. Explain how to call the different emergency services and when it's appropriate to call them. Emphasize the importance of following directions from an instructor for safety.

4. The first knot (15 minutes)

Using short lengths of parachord, teach the kids a very simple knot. I've found an overhand knot, Figure-of-eight and Reef knot are a good level for Beavers. Let them keep the cord to take it home and practice with.

Session 2: Building Pioneering Gadgets

Objective: Beavers will learn how to build pioneering gadgets using elastic band techniques and will construct their own pioneering gadgets.

Equipment Needed: Pioneering equipment (such as ropes, elastic bands, wooden poles), safety equipment (like gloves, safety glasses), step-by-step instructions for simple pioneering gadgets.

Activity Plan:

1. Elastic Band Techniques (20 minutes):

Demonstrate how to use elastic bands in pioneering gadget construction. Show how they can be used for binding and other functions in a gadget.

2. Gadget Construction (35 minutes):

Under supervision, allow Beavers to build their own pioneering gadgets using elastic band techniques. This could be a simple gadget like a miniature catapult or a tripod.

3. Review and Sharing (5 minutes):

Allow each Beaver to show their gadget and explain how they built it. This will allow them to take responsibility for their work and learn from each other's techniques.

After these sessions, encourage the Beavers to continue practising their pioneering skills and building more gadgets to fulfil the requirements for the Pioneering badge.

Adventure Skills – Hiking stage 1

Session 1: Preparing for a Hike and Basic Map Reading
Objective: Beavers will learn what to pack for a hike, appropriate attire, and the basics of map reading.

Equipment Needed: Backpacks, hiking gear (hats, water bottles, rain jackets, etc.), snacks, simple maps, and compasses.

Activity Plan:

1. Pack for a Hike Relay (15 minutes):
Set out a variety of items, both necessary and unnecessary for a hike. Beavers must race to pack a backpack with the correct items. Discuss why each item is necessary or unnecessary.

2. Dress for Success Relay (15 minutes):
Lay out a variety of clothing suitable for different weather conditions. Divide Beavers into teams and have them race to dress a team member in appropriate clothing for a given scenario.

3. Introduction to Map Reading (30 minutes):
Introduce Beavers to a simple map. Show them how to identify key features, such as hills, rivers, and trails. Let them practice reading the map and pointing out features.

Session 2: Hiking Safety and Practice Hike

Objective: Beavers will learn about hiking safety, including the Buddy system and distress signals. They will also go on a short, supervised hike.

Equipment Needed: Whistles, simple maps, and compasses.

Location: Meet at the local park or other suitable location for a short hike

Activity Plan:

1. Review of Hiking Safety (15 minutes):
Discuss the importance of following directions, staying on the trail, and staying with a buddy while hiking. Teach the main distress signals and let Beavers practice using their whistles.

2. Practice Hike (30 minutes):
Take Beavers on a short hike in a local park or woodland area. Encourage them to use their maps and pay attention to their surroundings.

3. Reflection and Sharing (15 minutes):
After the hike, have a group discussion about the experience. What did they enjoy? What was challenging? Did they remember to use their maps and stay with their buddy?

By the end of these two sessions, Beavers will be well-prepared for future hikes, understand the importance of safety while hiking, and have the knowledge they need to earn their Hillwalking badge. Remember to plan future hikes to fulfil the requirement of attending at least two hikes.

Adventure Skills – Emergencies stage 1

Session 1: Basic First Aid and Emergency Services
Objective: Beavers will learn the contents of a personal First Aid kit, basic First Aid rules, and about different emergency services.

Equipment Needed: Assorted First Aid items (band-aids, gauze, antiseptic wipes, etc.), pictures or examples of different emergency services.

Activity Plan:

1. Create a First Aid Kit (20 minutes):
Show the Beavers various items that could go in a personal First Aid kit. Have them assemble their own kit from these items, discussing the purpose of each one.

2. Basic First Aid Rules (15 minutes):
Discuss the basic rules of First Aid, such as always getting an adult, never moving someone who's seriously hurt, and washing hands before treating a cut. Use role-play to illustrate these rules.

3. Emergency Services Puzzle (25 minutes):
Introduce the different emergency services (police, fire, ambulance, coastguard) and when to call them. Make this interactive by creating a matching game or puzzle where Beavers must match the service with the correct scenario.

Session 2: Treating Minor Cuts and Emergency Reporting
Objective: Beavers will learn how to treat minor cuts and how to report an emergency properly.

Equipment Needed: First Aid kit, phone (or toy phone), role-play scenarios.

Activity Plan:

1. Treating Minor Cuts (20 minutes):
Demonstrate how to safely clean and bandage a minor cut using a First Aid kit. Beavers can practice on themselves or on a doll or stuffed animal.

2. Emergency Reporting Role Play (30 minutes):
Set up scenarios where an emergency has occurred, and the Beavers must 'call' for help. Using a toy phone, they should practise what to say to the operator, including their name, location, and description of the situation.

3. Personal Health and Safety Discussion (10 minutes):
Wrap up the sessions by talking about how Beavers can be responsible for their own health and safety, such as by following rules, wearing appropriate gear for activities, and practicing good hygiene.

After these two sessions, Beavers should have a good understanding of basic First Aid and know how to report an emergency, fulfilling the requirements for the Emergencies badge.

Adventure Skills – Air Activities stage 1

Session 1: Understanding Flight and Aircraft

Objective: Beavers will learn about different things that can fly, different types of flying machines, and the features of an airport.

Equipment Needed: Pictures of different flying things and aircraft, model or large picture of an airport, safety guidelines around aircraft.

Activity Plan:

1. Brainstorming Flying Things (15 minutes):

Start the session with a brainstorming activity. Ask Beavers to name all the things they know that can fly. This can include animals, natural phenomena, and man-made objects.

2. Discussion on Flying Machines (20 minutes):

Show pictures of different types of flying machines, such as aeroplanes, helicopters, hot air balloons, drones, etc. Discuss each type and ask Beavers to share what they know about them.

3. Understanding Airports (25 minutes):

Using a model or picture of an airport, discuss the different features such as the runway, terminal, and control tower. Explain the purpose of each feature.

Session 2: Paper Aeroplanes and Safety

Objective: Beavers will learn how to build a paper aeroplane that can fly, climb, and turn. They will also learn about safety around aircraft.

Equipment Needed: A4 sheets of paper, markers, safety guidelines around aircraft.

Activity Plan:

1. Building Paper Airplanes (30 minutes):

Demonstrate how to build a paper aeroplane from an A4 sheet. Let Beavers construct their own planes, and then have a competition to see whose aeroplane can fly the furthest, climb the highest, and turn the best.

2. Discussing Safety (25 minutes):

Discuss the importance of safety around aircraft. Talk about the risks and how to minimize them, such as not approaching an aircraft without permission, not running on the tarmac, etc.

3. Wrap-Up (5 minutes):

Reminding Beavers about what they've learned and encourage them to share their new knowledge with their families and friends. Mention that visiting an airport in person could be a great opportunity to see these principles in action, and to look out for them next time they have the opportunity.

Adventure Skills – Paddling stage 1

Session 1: Paddling Basics and Safety

Objective: Beavers will learn the basic parts of a kayak or boat, the importance of a wet suit, buoyancy aid, and life jacket, and understand the limits of where they can go when afloat.

Equipment Needed: Wet suit, buoyancy aid, life jacket, kayak or boat, pictures or examples of different paddling areas and wind conditions.

Activity Plan:

1. Wet Suit and Safety Gear Introduction (20 minutes):
Explain and demonstrate what a wet suit does and the importance of buoyancy aids and life jackets. Allow Beavers to try on and experience the gear.

2. Kayak or Boat Familiarization (15 minutes):
Show the Beavers a kayak or boat and point out the bow and stern. Let them explore the kayak or boat under supervision.

3. Paddling Limits Discussion (25 minutes):
Use pictures or maps to illustrate different paddling areas and explain the limits of where they can go when they are afloat. Discuss the reasons for these limits and the dangers of going beyond them.

Session 2: Weather Conditions, Emergency Services, and Practical Exercise

Objective: Beavers will learn about weather conditions for paddling, how to contact emergency services, and will take part in a short exercise afloat.

Equipment Needed: Pictures or examples of different wind conditions, phone (or toy phone), paddling gear, and a safe body of water for a short paddling exercise.

Activity Plan:

1. Weather Conditions Discussion (15 minutes):
Explain and show examples of different wind conditions, specifically what a Force 3 wind looks like. Discuss why it's unsafe to go afloat in such conditions.

2. Emergency Services Role Play (20 minutes):
Set up scenarios where an emergency has occurred while paddling, and the Beavers must 'call' for help. Using a toy phone, they should practice what to say to the operator, including their location and description of the situation.

3. Short Paddling Exercise (25 minutes):
Under close supervision and in a safe and controlled environment, let the Beavers go afloat in a kayak or boat. They should stay within the previously discussed limits and use the Buddy system.

After these two sessions, Beavers should have a basic understanding of paddling safety and have experienced going afloat, fulfilling the requirements for the Paddling badge.

Adventure Skills – Rowing stage 1

Session 1: Introduction to Rowing and Basic Boat Parts
Objective: Beavers will learn about the parts of a boat, the importance of a personal flotation device, the correct clothing for rowing, and how to assist in the launching of a small punt.

Equipment Needed: Small punt (rowing boat), personal flotation device, examples of rowing clothing, basic rowing theory materials (books, diagrams, etc.)

Activity Plan:

1. Introduction to the Rowing Boat (20 minutes):
Show the Beavers a small punt, pointing out the bow, stern, transom, port, and starboard. Explain the importance of each part and how they relate to rowing.

2. Safety Gear and Clothing (20 minutes):
Discuss the importance of a personal flotation device and demonstrate how to wear it properly. Discuss the correct clothing for rowing, emphasizing protection against the elements and water.

3. Launching a Punt (20 minutes):
Under supervision, allow the Beavers to assist with the launch of a small punt. Demonstrate each step and explain the importance of each action.

Session 2: Practical Rowing and Emergency Preparedness

Objective: Beavers will learn to row a small punt, understand the weather conditions for rowing, learn how to act in case of a capsized boat, and how to contact emergency services.

Equipment Needed: Small punt, oars, personal flotation device, rowing clothing, pictures or examples of different wind conditions, phone (or toy phone), safe body of water for rowing exercise.

Activity Plan:

1. Rowing a Punt (20 minutes):

With an instructor, allow each Beaver to row the small punt. This should be done in a safe and controlled environment, and the Beavers should be taught the basic rowing technique.

2. Weather and Safety (20 minutes):

Discuss the importance of understanding the weather conditions, especially wind, for rowing. Explain what a Force 4 wind looks like and why they shouldn't go afloat in such conditions.

3. Emergency Preparedness (20 minutes):

Discuss the importance of staying with a capsized boat and how to call for help. Explain how to recognize the limits of where they can go each time they go afloat for rowing.

Ensure the Beavers understand these concepts and practices. After these sessions, organize two additional half-day rowing exercises, ensuring a minimum of two hours afloat for each Beaver to fulfill the requirements for the Rowing badge.

Adventure Skills – Sailing stage 1

Session 1: Introduction to Sailing and Basic Sailing Theory

Objective: Beavers will learn about the basic parts of a sailing boat, the importance of a personal floatation device, the correct clothing for sailing, and basic sailing theory.

Equipment Needed: Sailing dinghy, personal floatation device, examples of sailing clothing, basic sailing theory materials (books, diagrams, etc.)

Activity Plan:

1. Introduction to the Sailing Boat (20 minutes):
Show the Beavers a sailing dinghy, pointing out the bow, stern, port, and starboard. Explain the importance of each part and how they relate to sailing.

2. Safety Gear and Clothing (20 minutes):
Explain the importance of a personal floatation device and show the Beavers how to wear it properly. Discuss the right clothing for sailing, emphasizing the need for protection against the elements and water.

3. Basic Sailing Theory (20 minutes):
Introduce the Beavers to basic sailing theory using simple diagrams and models. Explain how the wind interacts with the sails and how it affects the direction and speed of the boat.

Session 2: Practical Sailing and Emergency Preparedness

Objective: Beavers will assist with the launch and recovery of a dinghy, steer a straight course, learn about weather conditions for sailing, how to act in case of capsizing, and how to contact emergency services.

Equipment Needed: Sailing dinghy, personal floatation device, sailing clothing, pictures or examples of different wind conditions, phone (or toy phone), safe body of water for sailing exercise.

Activity Plan:

1. Launch and Recovery of a Dinghy (20 minutes):
Under supervision, allow the Beavers to assist with the launch and recovery of a sailing dinghy. Demonstrate each step and explain the importance of each action.

2. Steering a Course (20 minutes):
With an instructor, allow each Beaver to take the helm and steer a reasonably straight course. This should be done in a safe and controlled environment.

3. Emergency Preparedness (20 minutes):
Discuss the importance of staying with a capsized boat and how to call for help. Explain what a Force 4 wind looks like and why they shouldn't go afloat in such conditions.

Ensure the Beavers understand the limits of where they can go each time they go afloat for sailing. After these sessions, organize two additional half-day sailing exercises, ensuring a minimum of two hours afloat for each Beaver to fulfil the requirements for the Sailing badge.

Games Galore – Indoor and Easy to Organise

Games and physical activities are a cornerstone of any successful Beaver Scouts meeting. Not only do they help burn off energy and keep the Beaver Scouts active and engaged, but they also bring an element of fun and excitement that can set a positive tone for the start or end of a meeting.

Indoor games and easy to set-up activities can be particularly useful during poor weather conditions or when outdoor space is limited. They can also be great tools for changing the dynamic of a meeting if the kids start to get restless or bored. A well-timed game can re-energize the group, refocus their attention, and inject a fresh burst of enthusiasm into the proceedings.

In this chapter, I will suggest a variety of games and activities that are suitable for indoor environments and require minimal set-up time. These games will range from those suitable for larger groups to more intimate activities designed for smaller teams. No matter the size or makeup of your Beaver Scouts group, you now have, in your hands, an array of games at your disposal to keep the meeting lively and enjoyable.

Even the simplest games require some level of preparation. To ensure you're always ready to dive into a game, here are five things that you should always have on hand:

A whistle: Essential for getting attention and signalling the start or end of a game.

A timer or stopwatch: Many games require timing, and a stopwatch or a simple kitchen timer can do the trick.

A set of cones or markers: Useful for designating areas, marking boundaries, or creating paths.

Balls of various sizes: They can be used in a multitude of games and activities.

Bibs or vests of different colours: Handy for dividing the group into teams.

The primary goal of these games is to ensure that every Beaver Scout is having fun and feeling included. As you read through these lists, consider how each game might be adapted to suit the needs and abilities of your group. Enjoy the process - the sound of laughter is a sure sign of a successful Beaver Scouts meeting!

Larger Groups (10-30 Beavers)

Animal Tag: Everyone is an animal in the forest. When the 'hunter' (tagger) tags an animal, they freeze until another animal frees them.

Compass Dash: Call out compass points (North, South, East, West), and the Beavers dash to the corresponding side of the room.

Scouter Says: Like "Simon Says," but with Scouting actions (e.g., "Scouter says, 'Pitch a tent!'").

Nature Relay Race: Beavers pass a nature-themed item (pine cone, leaf, etc.) down the line, taking it in turns to go through their legs and over their head. For added fun – tie the object to a piece of string and get them to pass it through a piece of clothing. Now they are all tied together!.

Knot Tying Challenge: Divide the Beavers into teams. The first team to have all members tie a correct knot wins. Encourage those that have figured it out to help the others. Works best with overhand knots and figure-of-eight for Beavers.

Hot Potato, Camping Style: Pass around a "hot" campfire stone. Whoever has it when the music stops is out.

Dodgeball: A standard game of dodgeball but the ball represents a harmful element in the wilderness, such as a bear or snake.

Sleeping Bag Race: Like a sack race, but using sleeping bags instead.

Four Corners, Compass Edition: Label the corners of the room as North, South, East, and West. Everyone has to run to a corner. A Blindfolded Beaver then calls out a direction, and the Beavers in that corner are out. Now everyone who is still in runs to a different corner.

Leaf Blower: Each Beaver tries to keep their leaf in the air the longest by only blowing on it.

Camping Obstacle Course: Set up an obstacle course with camping tasks like setting up a mini tent, packing a bag, etc.

Musical Maps: Like musical chairs, but with maps of local parks or trails. When the music stops, the Beavers must stand on a map (you might want to have the Beavers make the maps as an activity first to save your nice ones for the hiking!).

Capture the Flag: Divide the Beavers into teams, each protecting their team's flag while trying to capture the other team's flag. Tuck a neckerchief into the back of the trousers to act as a "life" if someone from the other team grabs their necker, they are "out".

Tug-of-War: Whoever pulls the other team over the line first, wins.

Hiking Gear Scramble: Scatter camping gear around the room. Call out an item, and the Beavers race to find and bring it back to their team.

Scout Leader Whistle - To be played throughout the whole evening while other things are going on: When the whistle blows, Beavers must perform a particular Scout action, like salute or tie a knot.

Nature Bingo Run: Place pictures of nature items around the room. Call out items for Beavers to find and return to their bingo card.

Duck Duck Goose, Wilderness Edition: Play a game of duck, duck, goose but replace "duck" and "goose" with animals found in the wild.

Tree Tag: One person is "it" and can only tag others if they aren't touching a "tree" (designated areas or objects in the room). The Beavers can only stay next to a tree for 5 seconds before they have to move to another one. When they get to a tree, they have to start counting down from 5 immediately

Star Constellation Relay: Beavers recreate constellations using chalk or tape in a relay format, adding one star at a time, and working to re-create a picture.

Fun games for the whole evening

It can also be fun to set up a game that runs throughout the evening – or even a whole camp! This peg game was suggested by my auntie Janet as one that they have enjoyed in lots of different situations.

These games can carry on while other activities are taking place to provide a different "special sauce" element to make the evening more fun.

Covert Pegging

Objective: The goal of this game is to attach as many clothes pegs as possible to the leaders' clothes without being noticed.

Materials Required: Five coloured clothes pegs per lodge.

Setup: At the start of the meeting, each Beaver lodge is given five clothes pegs, each of a specific colour.

Rules Explanation: The Beavers are briefed on the game. They are told that their mission for the night is to attach these pegs to the clothes of the leaders without the leaders noticing. The Beavers can peg at any point throughout the evening - the game isn't played in one specific time slot, but rather throughout the entire meeting.

Strategy: Beavers are encouraged to devise stealthy strategies and work together as a lodge to distract the leaders or find the opportune moment to peg without getting caught.

Playing: Throughout the meeting, Beavers attempt to complete their mission. Leaders should act as they normally would, to provide a real challenge for the Beavers. However, leaders should also ensure they aren't making it impossible for Beavers to succeed - part of the fun is in seeing a peg successfully placed!

Scoring: At the end of the meeting, the leaders gather and count the number of pegs of each colour on their clothes.

Winning: The lodge with the most pegs successfully attached to the leaders wins the game.

Note: This game is a fun exercise in stealth and coordination, but it should also teach Beavers about respect for others' personal space.

Great fun! Not only does it require skill and strategy, but it also promotes teamwork and friendly competition.

Whispered Words

Objective: To pass a secret message from one lodge to another without being caught by the leaders.

Materials Required: None.

Setup: At the beginning of the meeting, each Beaver lodge is assigned a secret message or phrase.

Rules Explanation: The Beavers' goal for the night is to pass their lodge's message to as many other lodges as possible without the leaders overhearing them.

Strategy: Beavers can strategize and find clever ways to pass the message discretely. They may whisper it during a game, write it down, or even develop a secret sign language.

Playing: Throughout the meeting, Beavers attempt to pass their message to members of other lodges. Leaders should act as they normally would, but should also try to intercept the messages.

Scoring: At the end of the meeting, each lodge reports how many messages they received.

Winning: The lodge that successfully sent its message to the most lodges without getting intercepted by a leader wins.

Hidden Tokens

Objective: To find and collect as many hidden tokens as possible throughout the evening.

Materials Required: Small tokens or objects, such as marbles or plastic coins, enough for each Beaver to find a few.

Setup: Before the meeting, leaders hide tokens all around the meeting place.

Rules Explanation: The Beavers' goal for the evening is to find and collect as many tokens as possible. However, they must be stealthy, as if a leader sees them picking up a token, that token is added to the leaders pile.

Strategy: Beavers need to be observant and also come up with stealthy ways to collect the tokens. They could distract the leaders, work in pairs, or create diversions.

Playing: Throughout the meeting, Beavers hunt for the hidden tokens. Leaders continue their usual activities, but also keep an eye out for any suspicious activity.

Scoring: At the end of the meeting, Beavers count their collected tokens.

Winning: Overall – If the Beavers end up with more tokens than the leaders they win. To add a bit of competition between the children, you can also add the rule that The Lodge that has collected the most tokens wins.

These games encourage strategic thinking, teamwork, and observation skills while providing ongoing entertainment for the evening.

Smaller Groups (less than 10 Beavers)

Scouting Charades: Act out different Scouting activities, and the others have to guess what it is.

Leaf Race: Each Beaver blows a leaf along the ground to get it across a finish line.

Nature Scavenger Hunt: Give each Buddy pair of Beavers a list of nature items to find in the local park.

Human Knot: Beavers stand in a circle, reach across to hold hands with two others, and then try to untangle themselves without letting go of each other's hands.

Tent Building Race: Divide the group into teams, and see who can set up and take down a small tent the fastest. – Use cheap, easy to set-up tents so your good ones for Summer camp don't risk damage!

Chubby Bunnies: Each Beaver takes it in turns to add a marshmallow to their mouth and say "Chubby Bunnies". If they swallow, dribble or fail to say "Chubby Bunnies" they are out

Camping "Kim's" Game: Set out camping gear, let the Beavers study it, then cover it up and see how many items they can remember.

Knots Race: See who can tie a specific knot the fastest. Add a dash to the other end of the hall to keep the energy levels up. Simple knots like a reef knot or a figure of 8 work best with the Beavers

Map Drawing Competition: Beavers try to draw a map of a local park or trail from memory.

Shadow Puppets: Using a flashlight and their hands, Beavers make shadow puppets on the wall of a tent or other surface.

Pass the Water (outside!): Beavers pass water from one to another using cups with holes in them, trying to fill up a bucket at the end.

Bucket Ball: Toss a ball into a bucket. If it lands in, the Beaver stays in the game. The last Beaver left wins.

Marshmallow Catch: Toss marshmallows and try to catch them in your mouth.

Torch Tag: One Beaver with a Torch tries to tag the others by shining the light on them in a darkened hall. When they are pointing the light at them, they have to shout out the name of the "caught" Beaver, otherwise they are still "in".

Nature Art: Beavers gather natural materials and use them to make art.

Fire Starter Race: Beavers race to see who can start a fire the fastest using flint and steel.

Sardines: One Beaver hides, and the others look for them. When they find them, they hide with them until everyone is hiding in the same place.

Compass Challenge: Beavers must find certain locations using a compass.

Zip Bong: Players sit in a circle. One player starts by saying "zip" to pass the imaginary "zip" to the player on their right, or "bong" to pass it to their left. If a player says "boing", it reverses direction. The pace should be kept fast and players are out if they hesitate or make a mistake. What makes this game fun is that the kids are not allowed to show their teeth, or laugh. If they do, they are "out".

Wink Murder: One player is secretly chosen as the murderer and kills others by winking at them. When a player is winked at, they must count to five and then dramatically "die." The other players try to figure out who the murderer is before they're all "dead."

Nature Bingo: Create bingo cards with pictures of local wildlife or plants, and have the Beavers mark off what they find.

Spoon and Egg Race, Scouting Edition: Do a traditional spoon and egg race, but with a twist: the egg is a "precious nature artifact" that must be transported safely back to camp.

Whistle Echo: The leader whistles a tune and the Beavers must echo it back.

Tug of War: A classic game that needs little explanation. Perhaps the two teams are "bears" and "wolves" fighting over territory.

Scouting Pictionary: Similar to charades, but this time they draw.

Animal Sounds: Each Beaver is given the name of an animal which they keep secret. Everyone makes their animal's sound and tries to find their matching animals based on sound alone. (Give each animal to at least 2 Beavers!)

Hug a Tree: Blindfolded Beavers are led to a tree. They feel the tree and then are led back to the start. They then remove the blindfold and have to find their tree again.

Pass the Parcel, Survival Edition: In each layer of the parcel, include a small item of survival gear (like a match, a button compass, a piece of candy for energy) and a note explaining its use.

Jump the Creek: Two ropes represent the sides of a creek. Beavers must jump across without falling in. The creek gets wider each round.

Musical Sleeping Bags: Like musical chairs, but with sleeping bags.

Scouting Quiz: A simple quiz about Scouting history or local nature.

Leaf Blower: Beavers have to blow a leaf across a finish line using a straw.

Sign Language Name Game: Beavers spell out their name using sign language or morse code.

Nature Sensory Bag: Fill a bag with natural items (pinecone, feather, stone, etc.). Beavers reach in and try to identify the item without looking.

Firewood Gathering Race: Beavers race to gather twigs and small branches for a pretend fire.

Neckerchief Tag: Beavers form two teams. They tuck their neckerchiefs into the back of their trousers and then try and capture the other team's neckers without losing their own.

More Games – Outdoor and Wide Games

Wide Games are a storied tradition in Scouting, and for good reason. They offer an engaging and exciting way to learn and practice key Scouting skills, from navigation and strategy to teamwork and respect for nature, all within the context of an adventurous game.

Unlike the indoor or quick-setup games, Wide Games are more complex, sometimes involving multiple stages, objectives, or rules. They require a bit more planning and setup, but the rewards are definitely worth it. The games can take on the form of treasure hunts, rescue missions, or survival challenges, all tied together with a captivating storyline that will keep the Beavers engaged and excited.

Wide Games are typically played in larger outdoor areas, like fields, parks, or woodlands. This provides plenty of space for Beavers to run, explore, and engage with the natural environment. However, larger playing areas also mean we need to take extra precautions to ensure safety.

Here are some safety ideas to consider:

Scouter Placement: Having Scout Leaders placed strategically around the playing area allows for supervision of the game from different vantage points. This helps ensure all Beavers are safe and engaged in the game.

Defined Boundaries: Before the game starts, clearly define the boundaries of the playing area with the Beavers. This helps to prevent them from wandering off too far and keeps the game contained within a manageable area.

Buddy System: This age-old Scouting tradition is especially useful in Wide Games. Pair up the Beavers and have them promise to keep an eye on each other to encourage teamwork and mutual responsibility.

Briefing: Before starting the game, conduct a briefing. Explain the rules of the game, define the boundaries, and remind them of the importance of the Buddy System and listening to instructions.

Whistle Signals: Equip leaders with whistles and establish clear signals for different situations. For instance, one blow could mean 'Attention', two blows 'Come to me', and three blows could indicate an emergency. Teach the Beavers these signals and ensure they understand their importance.

Check-In Points: If the game area is particularly large, consider establishing check-in points where Beavers must report at set intervals. This can help in keeping track of everyone's whereabouts and ensuring all are safe and accounted for.

The key to a successful Wide Game is not just in its setup or storyline, but also in its execution. Your goal is to ensure every Beaver Scout has a great time while learning and growing.

The Lost Map

Backstory: A group of explorers lost their map in the wilderness, and the Beavers are the brave Scouts entrusted with the mission of finding it. The map is the only way to find the hidden treasure of the legendary Scout King.

Mechanics: The game master hides a "map" somewhere within the game area before the game begins. The Beavers are then divided into teams and given clues to locate the map. The first team to find the map wins.

Characters and Roles: Each team could have a navigator (reads the clues), a Scout (looks for the map), and protectors (defend their team from "wild animals" - other leaders acting as obstacles).

Equipment: Clues (written on paper), a map, costumes/masks for leaders acting as wild animals.

Ideal Size and Terrain: Suitable for 10-30 Beavers. Works best in a woodland area or a large field with hiding places.

Alien Invasion

Backstory: Aliens have invaded Earth, and the Beavers are the only hope for mankind. Their mission is to deactivate the alien's power source and save the planet.

Mechanics: The game master hides "alien power sources" (glow sticks or painted rocks) around the game area. The Beavers are split into teams and must find and collect the power sources. The team with the most power sources at the end of the game wins.

Characters and Roles: Each team could have seekers (who look for the power sources), carriers (who carry the power sources), and guards (who protect their team from the "aliens" - other leaders acting as obstacles).

Equipment: Glow sticks or painted rocks, costumes for leaders acting as aliens.

Ideal Size and Terrain: Suitable for 10-30 Beavers. Best played in a large open field or woodland area, especially if it can be played in the dark.

Pirate's Gold

Backstory: Pirate's Gold has been hidden on a deserted island, and the Beavers are the courageous adventurers on a quest to find it.

Mechanics: Leaders hide "gold" (painted rocks or gold foil-wrapped chocolates) around the game area. The Beavers, divided into crews, must find the gold. The crew with the most gold at the end wins.

Characters and Roles: Each crew could have a captain (directs the team), mates (search for gold), and a quartermaster (keeps count of the collected gold).

Equipment: "Gold" (painted rocks or gold foil-wrapped chocolates).

Ideal Size and Terrain: Suitable for 10-20 Beavers. A sandy area or beach would provide the perfect backdrop, but it could also be played in a field or woodland area.

Survivors and Rescuers

Backstory: A plane has crashed on a deserted island, and the Beavers are the survivors. Some of the Beavers are rescuers who have arrived to save the survivors.

Mechanics: Divide the Beavers into two groups - survivors and rescuers. The survivors are given a head start to hide within the game area. The rescuers then have to find and "save" the survivors.

Characters and Roles: The survivors (hide from the rescuers) and the rescuers (find and "save" the survivors).

Equipment: None.

Ideal Size and Terrain: Suitable for 10-30 Beavers. Works best in a large field or woodland area with hiding spots.

Survival Challenge

Backstory: The Beavers are adventurers who must survive in the wild and build a shelter before nightfall.

Mechanics: Beavers, in teams, are given materials and must build a 'shelter' (a structure made of sticks, ropes, etc.) within a set time. Leaders judge the shelters on stability, size, and creativity.

Characters and Roles: Each team could have 'builders' (to construct the shelter), 'gatherers' (to collect materials), and 'designers' (to plan the shelter).

Equipment: Sticks, ropes, and other natural materials.

Ideal Size and Terrain: Suitable for 10-20 Beavers. A woodland area with plenty of sticks and leaves is perfect.

Animal Rescue Mission

Backstory: The Beavers are part of an animal rescue team, and they have been tasked with saving endangered animals (stuffed toys) from a dangerous forest fire.

Mechanics: Leaders hide stuffed animals around the play area. Beavers, in teams, must follow clues to find the animals and bring them back to the 'rescue base' (a designated spot).

Characters and Roles: Each team could have 'navigators' (to follow clues), 'rescuers' (to retrieve animals), and 'medics' (to check animals' 'health' at the base).

Equipment: Stuffed animals, clues for navigation, first aid kit for 'medics'.

Ideal Size and Terrain: Suitable for 10-20 Beavers. A woodland area with various hiding spots is perfect for this game.

Quest for the Dragon's Egg

Backstory: A dragon has lost its egg in the mystical forest. The Beavers, as brave knights and wizards, must find and return the egg before it's too late.

Mechanics: A large ball (the dragon's egg) is hidden in the play area. Beavers, in teams, must solve riddles and complete challenges to find the egg and bring it back to the dragon's nest (a designated spot).

Characters and Roles: Teams could have 'riddle solvers', 'egg carriers', and 'defenders' to protect the egg from 'evil knights' (leaders trying to take the egg).

Equipment: A large ball or inflatable egg, riddles for navigation, costumes for leaders.

Ideal Size and Terrain: Suitable for 10-20 Beavers. A large park or woodland with hiding places works well for this game.

Time Travellers

Backstory: The Beavers have discovered a time machine and travelled back to the age of dinosaurs. They must collect dinosaur eggs (small balls or balloons) and bring them back to the future.

Mechanics: 'Dinosaur eggs' are scattered around the play area. Beavers, in teams, must find as many eggs as they can within a set time.

Characters and Roles: All Beavers are 'time travelers', with each team working together to collect eggs.

Equipment: Small balls or balloons as 'dinosaur eggs', time machine made from cardboard.

Ideal Size and Terrain: Suitable for 10-30 Beavers. An open field or large outdoor area is best for this game.

Mars Colony

Backstory: The Beavers are astronauts on Mars, and they must build a sustainable colony using available resources.

Mechanics: Beavers, in teams, are given materials (cardboard, tape, etc.) to build their 'Mars colony' (structures like habitats, greenhouses, etc.). Leaders judge the colonies based on creativity, stability, and team work.

Characters and Roles: Each team could have 'engineers' (to build), 'scientists' (to plan the colony), and 'explorers' (to gather additional resources).

Equipment: Cardboard, tape, and other building materials.

Ideal Size and Terrain: Suitable for 10-20 Beavers. A flat outdoor area is perfect for this game, but this one could be played indoors

Beaver Superheroes

Backstory: The Beavers are superheroes trying to save the world. A villain (played by a leader) has stolen the 'world energy crystal' and the superheroes must retrieve it.

Mechanics: The 'world energy crystal' (a shiny object) is hidden in the area. The Beavers, in teams, must complete a series of tasks or challenges to find the crystal.

Characters and Roles: Teams could have 'task solvers', 'crystal carriers', and 'defenders' to protect the crystal from the villain.

Equipment: A shiny object for the crystal, tasks or challenges, superhero capes for the Beavers.

Ideal Size and Terrain: Suitable for 10-20 Beavers. An open field or park is perfect for this game.

Explorers in the Jungle

Backstory: The Beavers are explorers on an expedition in the jungle. They must navigate through the jungle and reach the 'lost city' while avoiding various 'jungle dangers'.

Mechanics: The Beavers, in teams, must navigate through a course (the jungle) using various skills like balancing, crawling, etc. Leaders act as 'jungle dangers' trying to tag the explorers.

Characters and Roles: Each team could have 'navigators' (to lead the way), 'lookouts' (to watch for 'dangers'), and 'explorers'.

Equipment: Various equipment for the course like balancing beams, tunnels, etc.

Ideal Size and Terrain: Suitable for 10-30 Beavers. A large outdoor area with space for a course is ideal.

Arctic Adventure

Backstory: The Beavers are adventurers on a mission in the Arctic. They must rescue a 'lost explorer' (a leader) and bring them back to the 'base camp'.

Mechanics: The 'lost explorer' is hidden in the area. The Beavers, in teams, follow a series of clues to find the explorer and bring them back.

Characters and Roles: Each team could have 'navigators' (to follow the clues), 'rescuers' (to 'assist' the explorer), and 'base camp keepers' (to prepare a 'warm welcome' for the explorer).

Equipment: Clues for navigation, arctic explorer gear for the Beavers.

Ideal Size and Terrain: Suitable for 10-20 Beavers. A woodland or park with hiding places is perfect.

Arts and Crafts: Hands-on Activities for Beavers

Crafts have always held a special place in Scouting. They provide a change of pace from the more traditional Scouting activities and games, allowing our Beavers to tap into their creativity, develop fine motor skills, and bring home something tangible that symbolises their Scouting journey.

Crafting offers an excellent opportunity for less experienced Scouters to shine. With a bit of research and preparation, anyone can organise a craft station that sparks interest and encourages participation. Don't worry about perfection; it's all about fostering creativity, patience, and joy in making something with one's hands.

Craft activities can be a valuable tool in reinforcing the theme of the evening. If you're having a Pirate-themed night, your Beavers could craft their own pirate hats, treasure maps, or cardboard telescopes. For a Jungle-themed night, they could make animal masks, paper plate snakes, or even create a miniature jungle using twigs, leaves, and pebbles.

When organising craft activities, it's helpful to split the Beavers into small, manageable groups, or Lodges. This ensures each Beaver gets enough attention and guidance. It also encourages teamwork and cooperation as they work together on their crafts.

One practical way to manage craft activities is by setting up different 'stations' in your den or hall. Each station could have a different craft related to your theme, with all necessary materials and instructions. Beavers can rotate through the stations, providing variety and keeping engagement levels high.

Here's a list of ideas, relating back to the themes we came up with earlier.

Pirate Adventure

Treasure Maps: With aged paper (or coffee-stained regular paper for effect), crayons, and markers, the Beavers can create their own treasure maps. Encourage them to include landmarks and X marks the spot!

Pirate Hats: Using black construction paper, scissors, and a bit of glue, the Beavers can fashion their own pirate hats. Don't forget the skull and crossbones!

Space Explorers

Rocket Building: Using empty toilet paper rolls, coloured paper, and glue, they can create their own mini rockets. They can even add a cotton ball for a smoke effect!

Galaxy in a Jar: Mix cotton balls, glitter, and coloured water in a jar for a beautiful, homemade galaxy.

Superhero Squad

Superhero Badges: The Beavers can create badges using craft foam or card, representing their superhero identity.

Design Your Superhero Cape: Using old t-shirts or fabric, they can design their own superhero capes, adding symbols or initials.

Wild West

DIY Bandanas: With fabric markers and plain bandanas, they can create their cowboy attire.

Wanted Posters: Using paper, pencils, and their imagination, the Beavers can create wanted posters for fictional Wild West outlaws.

Under the Sea

Fish Crafts: Use paper plates, paint, and googly eyes to create colourful, unique fish.

DIY Jellyfish: Streamers, a paper bowl, and some creative colouring can transform into an adorable jellyfish.

Rainforest Expedition

Animal Masks: Create rainforest animal masks using paper plates, paint, and elastic.

Leaf Rubbings: With real leaves and crayons, the Beavers can create beautiful artwork while learning about different plants.

Castle and Knights

Design Your Shield: Using cardboard and paint, they can design a shield fit for a knight.

Create a Castle: Using recycled boxes and markers, the Beavers can construct their own castle.

Around the World

National Flags: Using coloured paper, the Beavers can recreate the flags of different countries.

Landmark Collages: By cutting pictures from magazines or printing from the internet, create collages of famous world landmarks.

Dinosaur Dig

Fossil Cookies: Using a simple salt dough and toy dinosaurs, the Beavers can create their own "fossil" cookies.

Paper Plate Dinosaurs: With paper plates, paint, and scissors, they can create their favourite dinosaurs.

Magical Creatures

Fairy Gardens: Using natural materials like twigs, leaves, and stones, the Beavers can create enchanting fairy gardens.

DIY Wands: Sticks, ribbons, and a little imagination can transform into a magic wand.

Mad Scientists

Invisible Ink: Using lemon juice and heat, the Beavers can create invisible messages.

Mentos and Coke: The classic explosion experiment – make sure you do it outside and be prepared for clean-up!

Garden Growers

Seed Planting: Provide the Beavers with a small pot, soil, and seeds to plant their own flowers or herbs.

Pinecone Bird Feeders: Pinecones, peanut butter, and birdseed make an easy and fun bird feeder.

Spy Academy

Code Breaking: Introduce the Beavers to simple ciphers and have them write secret messages.

Fingerprint Art: Using ink pads, the Beavers can make fingerprint pictures of their spy super team and its headquarters.

Time Travellers

Timeline Crafts: Using craft paper and markers, the Beavers can create timelines of important historical events or their own lives.

Historical Costume Hats: Using paper, they can design and construct hats from different historical periods.

Super Sleuths

Clue Hunt: Create a series of clues for the Beavers to find around your meeting place. They can be riddles, puzzles, or simple hints.

Ink Pad Fingerprints: Using ink pads and paper, Beavers can learn how to take and examine fingerprints.

Jungle Journey

Animal Masks: Using paper plates and craft supplies, the Beavers can create masks of their favorite jungle animals.

Jungle Vine Snake: Using green construction paper, googly eyes, and red tongue cutouts, they can create their own jungle snake.

Artists' Studio

Mini Canvas Painting: Provide mini canvases, paint, and brushes for the Beavers to create their own masterpieces.

Clay Sculptures: With air-dry clay, they can sculpt and paint a creation of their choice.

Circus Fun

Juggling Balls: Fill balloons with rice to create juggling balls that the kids can practice with.

Clown Hats: Using large construction paper, they can create and decorate their own clown hats.

Insect Inspectors

Bug Rubbings: Similar to leaf rubbings, you can create insect rubbings using toy insects and crayons.

Caterpillar Craft: Using pompoms, googly eyes, and craft sticks, the Beavers can create their own colourful caterpillars.

Fairy Tales

Puppet Making: Using paper bags, craft supplies, and a bit of imagination, Beavers can create puppets of their favourite fairy tale characters.

Castle Building: With cardboard boxes and craft supplies, the Beavers can create their own fairy tale castle – you might try this one as a team!

Sports Day

Team Banners: Using craft paper, markers, and stickers, the kids can create banners for their Sports Day teams.

Medal Making: Using cardboard, foil, and ribbon, they can make their own sports medals.

Farm Life

Butter Churning: With heavy cream and a jar, the Beavers can experience making their own butter.

Farm Animal Crafts: Using craft supplies, the Beavers can create their favourite farm animals.

Arctic Explorers

Igloo Building: Using marshmallows and toothpicks, the Beavers can construct their own mini igloos.

Polar Animal Crafts: Using craft supplies, they can create their favorite polar animals.

Island Survival

Message in a Bottle: Using paper, markers, and a bottle, the Beavers can write their own SOS messages.

DIY Rafts: Using popsicle sticks and glue, they can construct mini rafts.

Polar Express

Christmas Ornament Making: Using craft supplies, you can create Christmas ornaments to hang on their trees at home.

Snowflake Cutouts: Using white paper and scissors, they can make beautiful snowflakes.

Heroes of History

Wax Museum: Beavers can create a wax museum, where each Beaver chooses a historical figure to research and then portray in play-doh.

Historical Art: Beavers can create art inspired by a historical event or person.

Mountain Climbers

Mountain Collage: Using magazines or printed photos, Beavers can create a collage of different mountains.

DIY Snow Globes: Using a jar, distilled water, glycerin, glitter, and a small plastic figure, the Beavers can create their own snow globe.

Back to Nature

Nature Scavenger Hunt: Create a list of items for the Beavers to find in nature, such as a certain type of leaf, a rock, etc.

Leaf Rubbings: They can collect a variety of leaves and create rubbings with crayons and paper.

Dessert Chefs

No-Bake Cookie Making: Beavers can make simple no-bake cookies with ingredients like oatmeal, peanut butter, and chocolate.

Decorating Cupcakes: Bake cupcakes ahead of time and let the Beavers have fun with icing and decorations.

World of Music

Homemade Instruments: The Beavers can create their own music instruments using household items like cans, plastic containers, and rice for shakers.

DIY Music Posters: Using art supplies, Beavers can create posters for their favourite bands or musicians.

Cooking with Beavers

In the great outdoors, few things are as rewarding and enjoyable as cooking a meal from scratch. For young Beaver Scouts, it's not just about the fun they have while preparing the food, but also about the invaluable skills they learn along the way. When a Beaver Scout is involved in the process of creating their meal, they gain a greater appreciation for the food they eat and the work that goes into preparing it. And who knows, they might even be more inclined to try those nutritious vegetables they helped to cook!

With Beaver Scouts, there are numerous methods you can employ to get them involved in cooking, each one is a different experience and can be used in different situations.

Trangias: Lightweight and portable, Trangia stoves are a great way to introduce Beavers to cooking. They can learn to cook simple dishes like pasta or scrambled eggs.

Gas Stoves: A step up from the Trangia, gas stoves can be used for more complex meals. Safety is especially important here due to the flammable gas.

Open Fire: There's nothing quite like cooking over an open fire. Beavers can learn to toast marshmallows or cook hot dogs on a stick.

Dutch Ovens: These heavy pots can be placed directly in the fire or coals, and are perfect for slow-cooked meals like stews or chili.

Solar Ovens: An eco-friendly option, solar ovens use the sun's rays to cook food. This is a good opportunity to teach about renewable energy. You definitely need a sunny day for this one though, so have a back-up!

Rock Frying: Using a flat rock heated in the fire as a makeshift frying pan can fun.

Steam Pit: A traditional method of cooking, a steam pit involves digging a hole, lining it with rocks, and using the steam from heated water to cook food wrapped in leaves.

Stick Cooking: Cooking food on a stick over an open fire is a classic Scouting activity. It's simple, fun, and the results are often delicious!

When cooking with Beavers, it's important to think about safety. Here a few safety tips:

Supervision: Always ensure that Beaver Scouts are supervised when they are near a heat source or handling sharp utensils.

Keep a Safe Distance: Teach the Beavers to maintain a safe distance from hot surfaces and open flames.

Proper Handling of knives and utensils: Show the Beavers the correct way to handle cooking tools and equipment to avoid injury.

Fire Safety: Make sure the Beavers know how to extinguish a fire properly and understand the importance of never leaving a fire unattended.

Hygiene: Teach the Beavers about the importance of washing their hands before handling food and after touching raw meat to prevent the spread of bacteria.

By getting Beaver Scouts involved in cooking, you're not just making meals—you're making memories, and teaching valuable life skills. Here are some ideas to get you started.

S'mores

Cooking Method: Open Fire

Ingredients: 12 biscuits, 6 marshmallows, 1 chocolate bar

Steps: Each Beaver toasts a marshmallow over the fire until it's to their liking. Then, they sandwich the marshmallow and a piece of chocolate between two biscuits. Enjoy right away! For a better melt on the chocolate, you can wrap the whole thing in tin foil and cook it in the embers – expect some burnt ones, so do a few spares!

Vegetable Skewers

Cooking Method: Open Fire/Grill

Ingredients: 2 bell peppers, 2 courgettes, 1 punnet of cherry tomatoes, 1 red onion, olive oil, salt, and pepper

Steps: Cut the vegetables into chunks. Each Beaver can thread their vegetables onto a skewer. Brush the skewers with olive oil and season with salt and pepper. Cook the skewers over the open fire or on a grill, turning occasionally, until the vegetables are charred and tender.

Pasta with Tomato Sauce

Cooking Method: Gas Stove/Trangia

Ingredients: 500g of pasta, 1 jar of tomato sauce, grated cheese

Steps: Boil the pasta according to the package instructions. Heat the tomato sauce in a separate pot. Drain the pasta and mix in the sauce. Serve with a sprinkle of cheese on top.

Cheese Quesadillas

Cooking Method: Skillet/Grill

Ingredients: 6 tortillas, 2 cups shredded cheese

Steps: Place a tortilla on a skillet over medium heat. Sprinkle some cheese over half the tortilla, then fold it in half. Cook until the cheese is melted and the tortilla is crispy, then flip and repeat on the other side. Cut into wedges to serve.

Egg in an Orange

Cooking Method: Open Fire/Embers

Ingredients: 6 oranges, 6 eggs

Steps: Each Beaver cuts the top off an orange and scoops out the inside (they can eat it as they go or save it for later). Crack an egg into the hollowed-out orange, then replace the top of the orange. Place it in the embers of the fire for about 10 minutes or until the egg is cooked. The orange will burn, but the water in the skin will make it last long enough that the egg will cook through before it does.

Dampers

Cooking Method: Open Fire

Ingredients: 3 cups of self-rising flour, 1 cup of water

Steps: Mix the flour and water together to form a dough. Each Beaver gets a handful of dough and wraps it around a clean, wooden stick. Cook it over the open fire until it's golden brown. These can be eaten plain or with jam or honey.

Vegetable Skewers

Cooking Method: Open Fire/Grill

Ingredients: 2 bell peppers, 2 courgettes, 1 punnet of cherry tomatoes, 1 red onion, olive oil, salt, and pepper

Steps: Cut the vegetables into chunks. Each Beaver can thread their vegetables onto a skewer. Brush the skewers with olive oil and season with salt and pepper. Cook the skewers over the open fire or on a grill, turning occasionally, until the vegetables are charred and tender.

Fruit Kebabs

Cooking Method: No cook

Ingredients: Assortment of fruits such as grapes, pineapple, strawberries, banana slices, melon cubes

Steps: Each Beaver threads their chosen fruit onto a skewer. This can be enjoyed as is or with a side of yogurt for dipping.

Campfire Popcorn

Cooking Method: Open Fire

Ingredients: Popcorn kernels, oil, salt

Steps: In a fire-safe pot with a lid, heat some oil and add the popcorn kernels. Cover and shake the pot over the fire until the popping slows down. Remove from heat and let it sit for a minute to make sure all the popping is done. Sprinkle with salt and serve.

Baked Beans and Sausages

Cooking Method: Gas Stove/Trangia

Ingredients: 1 can of baked beans, 6 sausages

Steps: Cook the sausages in a pan until browned and cooked through. Heat the baked beans in a pot. Serve the sausages with the baked beans on the side.

Campfire Pizza

Cooking Method: Open Fire

Ingredients: Pizza base, pizza sauce, shredded cheese, a selection of toppings for the Beavers to choose from – Ham, sweetcorn, cooked chicken, pepperoni mushrooms etc

Steps: Each Beaver spreads pizza sauce on their base, then sprinkles cheese and their chosen toppings. Wrap the pizzas in foil and cook over the fire until the cheese is melted and the crust is crispy. Keep the pizza away from direct heat, the plan is a slow cook so that the cheese melts and the base doesn't burn.

Chocolate Bananas

Cooking Method: Open Fire/Embers

Ingredients: 6 bananas, 2 bags of chocolate buttons

Steps: Each Beaver makes a lengthwise cut into their banana, being careful not to cut all the way through. Stuff the cut with chocolate buttons, then wrap the banana in foil. Cook in the fire's embers for about 5-10 minutes until the chocolate has melted and the banana goes all squishy and gooey. Eat with a spoon.

All these recipes are designed to be simple and easy to do with Beavers. The key here is that they have fun and get the experience of cooking, not that they eat everything. It is their parent's job to argue with them about whether they like mushrooms. It is your job to inspire them and make sure they love coming to Beavers, while hopefully teaching them one or two things along the way.

I have found that cooking with Beavers is an amazing activity both on camp and on evenings in the hall. Just the fact that they have been involved in the preparation of the food, they've used dangerous things like fire and knives, and the peer pressure of the fact that everyone else is eating it can help even quite fussy Beavers to try new things that they would not have tried if they were just presented on a plate.

The Magic of the Campfire

There's something truly enchanting about the campfire on the Saturday evening of a weekend camp. After a day filled with adventure and learning, everyone comes together in the gentle glow of the fire. It's a time for song, for laughter, for stories, and for shared experiences. It's a time that weaves together the many threads of Scouting into a beautiful tapestry of fellowship and fun.

The campfire is more than just a gathering; it's a performance, a ceremony, and an embodiment of the spirit of Scouting. At the heart of it all is the Campfire Chief. This individual, often a leader, but sometimes a capable and experienced older Scout, serves as the master of ceremonies. It is their role to guide the energy of the group, to lead the songs, to ensure everyone is included, and to create an atmosphere of fun, respect, and camaraderie.

The Campfire Chief understands the rhythm of a good campfire. The energy ebbs and flows, moving from boisterous laughter and silly songs to quieter moments of reflection. The programme of the campfire can be planned or played by ear. Starting with high energy to engage and excite the Beavers, moving through skits and songs that get everyone up and moving, and involved, then gradually moving towards quieter, more reflective activities as the evening draws to a close works really well.

Songs and skits are the lifeblood of the campfire. They bring joy, foster a sense of belonging, and provide an opportunity for Beavers to step into the spotlight and share something with their friends. Everyone participates, everyone contributes, and everyone is part of the magic. You will find that quite shy and retiring Beavers can really come out of their skins when it comes to the campfire. If you get the set-up right, you can find budding thespians and entertaining performers that you had no idea existed in your group. Last year at our group summer camp, one of the quieter Cubs, Jude, found his voice. He performed in five or six skits, and I had to ask him to sit down for a while to let some of the other kids have a go. He found a love of performing that he might never have come across without that campfire. Who knows where it will take him, but it could open doors that may have stayed closed otherwise. That introduction to performing in front of people at a campfire is a huge part of the reason why I am now comfortable speaking in front of large rooms of people, which is a skill that helps in so many aspects of my career and business.

Skits are a core part of the campfire too. They can be individual, or groups, long (up to a 3 or 4 minutes) or just a few seconds. Getting the kids to practice their skits in their lodges can be a fun activity during the day ahead of the performance in the evening. My favourite skit, the one that I am known for in my group, is Cecil the caterpillar, which goes like this.

I start with my normal voice

James - "Cecil is a caterpillar, Cecil is my friend, the first time I saw Cecil, he was this big (hold up two fingers showing the size of a normal caterpillar)

Audience – How big?

James – This big (holds up the two fingers again)

I said "Cecil, what have you done?" he said "I've eaten a whole cabbage leaf!"

I said "Cecil – you are naughty!"

A nice quiet start, but it's going to get interesting...

James (putting on a slightly higher pitched voice and a bit more babyish) – "Thethil is a caterpillar, Thethil is my fwiend, the nectht time I thaw Thethil, he was thith big (hold up two fingers showing the size of a really big caterpillar – about 10cm)

Audience – How big?

James – Thith big (holds up the two fingers again)

I thaid "Thethil, what have you done?" he thaid "I've eaten a whole cabbage!"

I said "Thethil – you are naughty!"

Now it starts to get a bit sillier. Carrying on in the same vein, and getting increasingly shriller and more babyish, I go through the skit with

"Eaten all the cabbages in the vegetable plot"

"All the cabbages in Castleknock"

"All the cabbages in Dublin"

"All the cabbages in Ireland"

"All the cabbages in Europe"

"All the cabbages in the world"

"All the cabbages in the whole Universe"

By the time I'm at "Europe" I'm moving from one side of the campfire to the other to show the enormity of this caterpillar, my voice is high and shrill, I have a ridiculous lisp and am blowing raspberries and quite red in the face.I'm jumping up and down to show how angry I am with this naughty caterpillar.

I keep going, making the performance more and more ridiculous. To show how big this caterpillar is now getting, I am running to one end of the area and holding out my left hand to show one end of him, then running 20 metres away to show the other end. When the audience shout "how big?". Instead of starting at the tail end where I am, I make a big show of running back to the beginning, showing where his head is, and then running back to the tail end.

By the "universe" section I'm often in the next field, out of breath and shouting THIIIITTTTHHHHH BBBBIIIIIIIGGGG at the top of my voice like a deranged toddler.

After the "universe" verse, I return to the campfire for the punchline:

James (normal voice, but keeping the lisp) - "Thethil is a caterpillar, Thethil is my fwiend, the necht time I thaw Thethil, he was thith big (hold up two fingers showing the size of normal caterpillar again)

Audience – How big?

James (sad) – Thith big (holds up the two fingers again)

I thaid "Thethil, what have you done?" he thaid "I was thick!"

The kids love it, and so do I. It's a skit that I learned as a Cub Scout from someone else (I'm afraid I can't remember who, it may have been my auntie Janet), and I have made it my own over the years. I put an enormous amount of energy into the performance, and it has kids and Scouters laughing every time. The contrast with the serious Group Scout Leader that they know most of the time and the idiot running from one end of a field to another in physical discomfort just to show the size of an imaginary caterpillar is so ridiculous.

Not all skits are as big and daft as "Cecil" our Scout leader Frank, does a great one about a button factory, and very often the kids will make up skits that have no real punchline. They can be desperately funny to the performers, but leave everyone else scratching their heads. It doesn't matter, everyone enjoys them, and you are teaching the kids that it's OK to stand in front of people and express yourself, the world doesn't end – in fact it gets a little bit better and easier to navigate. What a life lesson!

The campfire is more than just a fire; it's a living, breathing part of the Scout experience. It's a tradition that connects us to generations of Scouts who came before us, and it's a memory that will stay with us long after the last embers have faded. As the Beavers troop off to bed, they carry with them the warmth and joy of the campfire, the echo of laughter and song, and the magic of a shared experience under the stars.

If you haven't done it before, getting involved in a campfire can be quite daunting. Hopefully your group will have an experienced Scouter who is happy to lead the campfire, in which case your job is to join in (yes –even new leaders sing and perform too!) and encourage the kids. However, if you do not have that experienced leader, here are a list of ideas for songs and skits that I love and enjoy.

Songs

You will have your favourites as I have mine, make it your own and have fun with it. Some songs (like the quartermaster's stores) will allow kids to jump in making up their own verses.

Campfire's Burning:

Campfire's burning, campfire's burning,
Draw nearer, draw nearer,
In the gloaming, in the gloaming,
Come sing and be merry.

Note: This song is usually sung in a round, meaning one group starts and the next group starts the song when the first reaches the second line, and so on.) The word "gloaming" means the time of day immediately following sunset – the kids may well ask you that)

The Grand Old Duke of York

He had ten thousand men,
He marched them up to the top of the hill,
And he marched them down again.
And when they were up, they were up.
And when they were down, they were down.
And when they were only halfway up,
They were neither up nor down.

(Actions: On the words "up," stand up; on "down," sit down; on "halfway up," crouch/squat. This can get quite lively as the song is usually sung faster and faster.)

The Quartermaster's Stores
(Chorus)

My eyes are dim, I cannot see,
I have not brought my specs with me,
I have not brought my specs with me.
Verse
There are rats, rats, as big as alley cats,
In the stores, in the stores
There are rats, rats, as big as alley cats,
In the Quartermaster's stores (kids' shout "Behind the door").
(Chorus)
Verses:
There were snakes, snakes, Big as garden rakes,
There were bats, bats, Wearing Scouters' hats,
There were bugs, bugs, Crawling on the rugs,
There were mice, mice, Running through the rice,
There were frogs, frogs, Jumping on the logs,

Baby Shark

Baby shark, doo doo doo doo doo doo,
Baby shark, doo doo doo doo doo doo,
Baby shark, doo doo doo doo doo doo,
Baby shark!

(Continue with "Mama shark," "Daddy shark," "Grandma shark," "Grandpa shark," and finally, "Let's go swim" and "Run away...". Each verse is accompanied by hand actions representing the different sharks.)

Molly Malone

In Dublin's fair city,
Where the girls are so pretty,
I first set my eyes on sweet Molly Malone,
As she wheeled her wheelbarrow,
Through streets broad and narrow,
Crying, "Cockles and mussels, alive, alive, oh!"

Chorus:
"Alive, alive, oh,
Alive, alive, oh",
Crying "Cockles and mussels, alive, alive, oh".

She was a fishmonger,
And sure 'twas no wonder,
For so were her father and mother before,
And they each wheeled their barrow,
Through streets broad and narrow,
Crying, "Cockles and mussels, alive, alive, oh!"

(Chorus)

She died of a fever,
And no one could save her,
And that was the end of sweet Molly Malone.
Now her ghost wheels her barrow,
Through streets broad and narrow,
Crying, "Cockles and mussels, alive, alive, oh!"

The Rattlin' Bog

Ho, ro, the rattlin' bog,
The bog down in the valley-o,
Real bog, the rattlin' bog,
The bog down in the valley-o.

And in that bog there was a hole,
A rare hole, a rattlin' hole,
And the hole in the bog and the bog down in the valley-o.

(Chorus)

And in that hole there was a tree,
A rare tree, a rattlin' tree,
And the tree in the hole and the hole in the bog,
And the bog down in the valley-o.

And on that tree there was a branch....

And on that branch there was a twig...

And on that twig there was a nest...

And in that nest there was an egg....

And in that egg there was a bird....

Boom Chicka Boom
Leader: I said a Boom Chika Boom
Group: I said a Boom Chika Boom
Leader: I said a Boom Chika Boom
Group: I said a Boom Chika Boom
Leader: I said a Boom Chika Rocka Chika Rocka Chika Boom
Group: I said a Boom Chika Rocka Chika Rocka Chika Boom
Leader: Uh huh
Group: Uh huh
Leader: Oh yeah
Group: Oh yeah
Leader: One more time...
Group: One more time
Leader - **Motorbike Style**: I said a Vroom Chika Vroom (Action: Revving a motorcycle)
...
Race Car Style: I said a Zoom Chika Zoom (Action: Pretend to be driving a fast car)
Opera Style: I said a Boom Chika Boom (Sung in an exaggerated, operatic way)
Janitor Style: I said a Broom Sweep'a Broom (Action: Pretend to be sweeping the floor)
Train Style: I said a Choo Chika Choo (Action: Move arms like a train conductor pulling
Gardener Style: I said a Bloom Chika Bloom (Action: Pretend to water flowers)
Chef Style: I said a Spoon Chika Spoon (Action: Pretend to stir a large pot)

B-I-N-G-O

There was a man who had a dog,
And Bingo was his name-o.
B-I-N-G-O,
B-I-N-G-O,
B-I-N-G-O,
And Bingo was his name-o.

Verse 2:
(Replace the first letter of the dog's name with a clap)
(clap)-I-N-G-O,
...
(clap)-(clap)-N-G-O,
...
(clap)-(clap)-(clap)-G-O,
...
(clap)-(clap)-(clap)-(clap)-O,
...
(clap)-(clap)-(clap)-(clap)-(clap),

On Top of Spaghetti

On top of spaghetti,
All covered in cheese,
I lost my poor meatball,
When somebody sneezed.

It rolled off the table,
And on to the floor,
And then my poor meatball,
Rolled out of the door.

It rolled down the garden,
And under a bush,
And then my poor meatball,
Was nothing but mush.

A hundred years later,
A meatball tree grew,
And now my poor meatball,
Is back in a stew

So if you eat spaghetti,
All covered with cheese,
Hold on to your meatball,
Whenever you sneeze.

Found a Peanut

Found a peanut, found a peanut, found a peanut yesterday,
Yesterday I found a peanut, found a peanut yesterday.

Cracked it open, cracked it open, cracked it open yesterday,
Yesterday I cracked it open, cracked it open yesterday.

It was rotten, it was rotten, it was rotten yesterday,
Yesterday it was rotten, it was rotten yesterday.

Ate it anyway, ate it anyway, ate it anyway yesterday,
Yesterday I ate it anyway, ate it anyway yesterday.

Got a stomachache, got a stomachache, got a stomachache yesterday,
Yesterday I got a stomachache, got a stomachache yesterday.

Called the doctor, called the doctor, called the doctor yesterday,
Yesterday I called the doctor, called the doctor yesterday.

Died anyway, died anyway, died anyway yesterday,
Yesterday I died anyway, died anyway yesterday.

Went to heaven, went to heaven, went to heaven yesterday,
Yesterday I went to heaven, went to heaven yesterday.

Gin Gang Gooly

Ging gang goolie goolie goolie goolie watcha,
Ging gang goo, ging gang goo.
Ging gang goolie goolie goolie goolie watcha,
Ging gang goo, ging gang goo.

Heyla, heyla sheyla,
Heyla sheyla, heyla ho.
Heyla, heyla sheyla,
Heyla sheyla, heyla ho.

Shally wally, shally wally, shally wally, shally wally,
Oompah, oompah, oompah, oompah.

Repeat.
This song is typically sung in a round with groups starting at different times.

Skits

Here are some ideas for skits that the kids (and Scouters) can do. The best way to prepare a skit is to make it an activity on the camp. Give the kids half an hour in the afternoon before the campfire to come up with a skit in their lodges. You can give them prompts like these, or just let them free flow-it.

The Invisible Bench: A few Beavers pretend to sit on an invisible bench. When the last Beaver comes along and is told about the invisible bench, they reply "But I moved the bench over there!" causing everyone to fall down.

Is It Time Yet?: One Beaver sits pretending to read a book. Other Beavers keep coming up and asking "Is it time yet?" The Beaver checks their watch and says "No, not yet." Finally, they say "Yes, it's time." and all Beavers run off stage.

The Echo: A Beaver shouts into an imaginary canyon and their echo (another Beaver behind the scenes) repeats it. Eventually, the echo starts answering before the Beaver shouts.

The Sweet Shop: Beavers take turns pretending to be customers and the shopkeeper. Each Beaver asks for a sweet with a silly name like Spider sugar, Crab Crackers, or Kangaroo Candy, then they crawl like a spider bounce off like a Kangaroo or walk on their hands backwards and sideways like a crab to leave the performance area.

Run-Ons: Short, funny skits or jokes that "run on" between longer skits. For example, a Beaver runs on stage, stops, looks at their watch, and says, "Oh, it's not time yet!" then runs off. They do this several times between songs, then finally say "It's time!" and everyone else runs on stage.

The Magic Bandana: One Beaver uses a bandana to do magic tricks, but the tricks always go wrong in a humorous way.

The Camping Trip: Beavers mime setting up camp, with each action going comically wrong.

The Fishing Trip: Beavers pretend to fish, but they keep pulling out ridiculous items.

The Fortune Teller: A Beaver pretends to tell fortunes, but all their predictions are humorously mundane. The last Beaver asks for their fortune and the fortune teller says, "I predict you will get up and leave." When the Beaver asks why, the fortune teller replies, "Because the skit is over."

The Lost Lollipop: One Beaver cries over a lost lollipop. Another Beaver tries to help them find it, but when they do, the first Beaver says, "Ew! It's all covered in dirt now!" and throws it away.

The Lost Beaver: A Beaver pretends to be lost and asks other Beavers for directions. Each gives them different, confusing instructions. Finally, the lost Beaver says, "Maybe I should just use my GPS," and walks off.

The Time Machine: Beavers pretend to use a time machine. They visit funny historical events, like the invention of the whoopee cushion. When they return to the present, one Beaver asks, "So, what did we learn?" The reply: "That we need better material for our next skit!"

The Uncooperative Canoe: Scouts pretend to be paddling a canoe but keep getting stuck. Finally, one Scout says, "Maybe we should have put it in the water!"

We’re going on a Bear Hunt: A repeat-after-me style skit where the leader narrates a bear hunt and the Scouts mime the actions.

We're goin' on a bear hunt,
We're going to catch a big one,
What a beautiful day!
We’re not scared,
(Action: March in place)

Uh-oh! Grass!
Long, wavy grass.
We can't go over it,
We can't go under it,
Oh no! We've got to go through it!
(Action: wooshy swooshy, wooshy swooshy)

(Chorus repeats)

Uh-oh! A river!
A deep, cold river.
We can't go over it,
We can't go under it,
Oh no! We've got to swim through it!
(Action: swim swim)

(Chorus repeats)

Uh-oh! Mud!
Thick, oozy mud.
We can't go over it,
We can't go under it,
Oh no! We've got to go through it!

(Action: gloop, gloop)

(Chorus repeats)

Uh-oh! A forest!
A deep, dark forest.
We can't go over it,
We can't go under it,
Oh no! We've got to go through it!

(Action: Stumble, trip, stumble, trip)

(Chorus repeats)

Uh-oh! A snowstorm!
A swirling, whirling snowstorm.
We can't go over it,
We can't go under it,
Oh no! We've got to go through it!

(Action: "Whooooosshh" sounds like the wind)

(Chorus repeats)

Uh-oh! A cave!
A narrow, gloomy cave.
We can't go over it,
We can't go under it,
Oh no! We've got to go through it!
(Action: Pretend to be carefully moving forward, arms out in front of you)

(Chorus repeats)
What's this?
Furry coat
Glinting eyes
Wet nose
We found the bear! (Roar!)
Quick!
Back through the cave (moving carefully)
Back through the snowstorm (whoosh, whoosh)

Back through the forest (stumble trip, stumble trip)
Back through the mud (gloop, gloop)
Back through the river (Swim Swim Swim)
Back through the grass (wooshy swooshy, wooshy swooshy)!
Back through the door
Run up the stairs
Into bed and under the covers
Back out of bed
Back down the stairs
Close the door!!!!
Back up the stairs
Back into bed
We're not going on a bear hunt again!

(Action: Reverse all the previous actions as you 'run' home)

Note: This is brought to life and illustrated by Michael Rosen and Helen Oxenbury in their book by the same name if you want a visual accompaniment for the story)

Jokes and Party Pieces

Campfires are not just about singing songs and performing skits; they also provide a unique platform for individual contributions that add a personal touch to the evening. These contributions can take many forms and offer each participant the chance to shine in their own way. For instance, if a leader plays the guitar, they could provide a musical interlude or accompany a song. This not only adds variety to the programme but can also encourage others to share their musical talents.

For those who are more comfortable with words than with music, humorous poetry or short, funny monologues can provide entertainment. A leader could recite a whimsical limerick or a Beaver could share a funny poem they've learned at school.

Jokes and party pieces also play a big part in campfire fun. Each Beaver could come prepared with their favourite joke to share with the group. Alternatively, they could perform a party trick, such as a magic trick, a funny impersonation, or a silly dance.

A Beaver might stand up and say, "Why don't we ever tell secrets on a farm? Because the potatoes have eyes, the corn has ears, and the beans stalk!" Or a leader might surprise everyone by doing an impressive impersonation of a famous person.

These individual contributions help to keep the campfire lively and engaging, and they give everyone the chance to take part in a way that suits their interests and abilities. By encouraging individual contributions, we foster a sense of community and make everyone feel valued and included.

Here are a couple of my favourite jokes that appeal to the sense of humour of 6-8 year olds and tend to get the ideas flowing. Yes – they are a little silly, and even a little rude, but that's what kids like, and I can't think of a better place and time to explore the boundaries of what is and is not appropriate that in a loving, caring environment with leaders and who can guide the themes and show the kids where the boundaries are in their culture:

Knock Knock

Who's there?

I diddup

I diddup who?

(say it out loud, it get's a laugh every time)

Q - What's brown and sticky?

A – A Stick

Winding up the campfire

As the campfire begins to dwindle, casting flickering shadows on the faces of weary but contented Beavers, it's time to change the tempo of the evening. The high-energy songs and lively skits give way to a quieter, more reflective mood. This transition is a magical moment, as the last of the day's energy fades into a calm and peaceful tranquility.

Gin Gang Gooly, sung at a slowing pace, can be a wonderful way to initiate this shift in energy. Its familiar tune and repetitive lyrics make it easy for the Beavers to join in, even as their attention starts to drift towards the lure of their sleeping bags. As the song ends, the transition to the quieter phase of the campfire is complete. The Beavers' voices soften, their movements slow, and the excitement of the day gives way to a serene calm. The emphasis now is on rest and reflection, rather than activity and noise.

Campfire's Burning is an ideal song to finish with. Its gentle tune and soothing lyrics can be sung softly, allowing the Beavers to wind down further. As the song draws to a close, the Beavers can continue to hum or sing the tune quietly to themselves as they begin to make their way back to their tents, the melody acting as a lullaby guiding them towards sleep.

Some leaders prefer to end the campfire with Taps, a traditional Scout song that encapsulates the sense of peace and tranquility that comes with the end of the day. Its simple, poignant lyrics are a fitting end to a day of adventure and camaraderie.

Others may choose to end the evening with a moment of quiet reflection, or share their favourite moment from the camp with in a "Scout's own" type moment. This can be a time for the Beavers to think about the day they've had, the fun they've shared, and the memories they've made. It's a moment to appreciate the beauty of nature, the warmth of the fire, and the company of friends.

We have recently started a tradition, tweaked from a suggestion from another Scout group where, as the Beavers head off to bed and walk past the campfire, they are given a small amount of sugar from the “memories jar”. As they throw it onto the fire, and the sugar sparkles and crackles, we encourage them to think of their favourite memory from the camp so far, and take it to bed with them.

Whichever way you choose to end your campfire the final moments of the campfire are a time for rest and relaxation, a chance for the Beavers to unwind and prepare for a good night's sleep, ready for the adventures that await them in the morning.

Making your Scouting journey your own

I want to finish with a few stories about my own Scouting journey to show how everyone's journey is different. These unique and personal elements truly bring Scouting to life. It's the rich tapestry of individual experiences, traditions, and shared moments that make Scouting such a rewarding journey, not just for the young Beavers but also for the Scouters who guide them.

Scouting provides a robust and well-structured framework, with a clear set of guidelines and a wealth of activities, but it is also flexible enough to allow for personal interpretation and innovation. This is where the magic of Scouting truly lies, in the personal touches, the beloved traditions and rituals, the shared laughter over a game, the joy of a festive gathering, the thrill of a fundraising challenge, and the camaraderie built over countless adventures.

Fundraising

Some groups are lucky, they are in relatively well-off areas or past generations have managed to build and hold on to a Scout den over the years. Others have to struggle every year to stay in operation.

Nowadays in western countries, there are lots of ways to receive grants and support, but you can also raise money yourselves. Our Scout group is on a mission to raise funds to buy a piece of land and build our own Scout den. Part of the inspiration for writing this book is that I would like to donate some of the proceeds to that cause. But there is a lot more to our plan. We have been lobbying with local politicians, raising our profile in the community and raising funds.

Last year the annual 5k run moved from a local school to the heart of the village. We took the opportunity to set up a stand right next to the finish line to raise money for the den. We bought sweets, fruit and drinks in bulk and packaged them up in little bags to sell to the other children in the village. We then set the

Beavers, Cubs and Scouts to work, making up the bags and then selling them with a credit card machine and taking cash. They loved it! It raised our profile in the community, gave the kids a life lesson about business and selling and raised €1,200 for the den.

Later in the year we organised a table quiz in the local tennis club which raised over €3,000 and brought most of the local politicians along. We also attended a Christmas fair, which had it's challenges, but with a bit of re-planning late in the day, also raised over €1,000. These kinds of activities do take a good bit of work, but they are also great fun, and much more enjoyable than sitting watching yet another Netflix series every evening. You and your fellow Scouters will get to know each other better, and you can bring a whole extra dimension to the group.

When I was a Venture Scout back in England in the 1990s, we did something similar – we waited tables at an event at the local cricket club to raise money for a trip to the Kandersteg international Scout centre in Switzerland. I've never waited on a table before or since, but I learned a new skill, had fun with my friends, and we went on the trip of a lifetime to that amazing Scouting centre in the heart of the Alps.

Community Profile

Another of the traditions that I've managed to bring over the Irish Sea from High Wycombe to the outskirts of Dublin is the annual Sleigh Run. Every year, at Christmas we'd dust off a homemade Santa Sleigh that someone had made years before, stick it on a trailer behind a car and go around the town with very loud Christmas music, and Santa Claus sitting in the back of the sleigh. We were all dressed in Christmas paraphernalia with santa hats and reindeer antlers giving out little bags of sweets to everyone who came out to see us.

Inside the bag was a little note saying "Happy Christmas from the Treadaway Explorer Scouts". Anyone who tried to give us money wasn't allowed to, we were just having fun and spreading Christmas spirit, not fundraising.

In 2021, I got my DIY tools out, and took advantage of the fact that my extremely handy brother-in-Law, Martin was over visiting us to build our own Santa's Sleigh using Frank's Trailer. We couldn't do the sleigh run that year because of Covid, but on the 16th December 2022, Castleknock Beavers, Cubs and Scouts did our very own version of the Sleigh run around our village. Complete with Garda escort, and all the new Scouters that we'd recruited over the year. Brilliant fun!

Fun for the Scouters too

Scouting is about making memorable experiences and learning opportunities for the kids, but I firmly believe that it's about the Scouters too. Without adults involved, groups die. And unless those adults are having fun, they will lose interest and drop out, and then all the experience that they have built up will be lost to the group forever.

Every month that passes is another month of experience for new leaders, and over a couple of years, people grow from having no idea about how to run a meeting or a camp, to experienced leaders with tried and tested techniques and ideas of their own. Scouting should be about coaching and mentoring each other just as much as it is about teaching the kids. When we're doing knots with the Cubs, I'm just as likely to be teaching a new Scouter a bowline, as to be teaching it to one of the Cubs. Once they have mastered the skill, they will pass it on to many more people than I can do on my own, and the skills will proliferate and grow through the group, the county, the province and the country.

We also do adult-only activities. We ran “starter camp” only last weekend for people who hadn’t been on a Scout camp in years, or ever. A Christmas meal in a local restaurant is a lovely way to relax, and a planning meeting in the pub can be a much more entertaining way to spend the evening than yet another episode of “Gogglebox”.

Our own traditions

Scouting traditions are brilliant, and they are even better when you put your own angle on them. My Mum kept all my badges from when I was a Cub, and I kept the ones from being a Scout and a venture Scout. They now proudly adorn my camp blanket, which I wear around the campfire, and which fascinates the kids as they ask questions about all the different places I've been and experiences I've had in Scouting.

Another tradition that we're going to bring in is a camp log. Brian's idea, from when he was a Scout. We're going to have a book for the group that someone will write up, draw pictures in and add printed photos to every time we go away. We'll get everyone who attended to sign it at the end of the camp, and that will be there for us to look back on in years to come.

Alongside the "Memory dust" idea that I talked about earlier, I also learned a couple of other super traditions from other Group Leaders when I completed my Group Scout Leader training. One Scout group uses a bell on camp to assemble everyone when it's time for an activity or to eat – we now have a bell.

On that same day, I also picked up the idea to change the way we view teddy bears on camp. We now encourage our Beavers to pick a "camp mascot" teddy bear that will come on camp with them. This solves the problem of them risking losing a favourite that they would not be able to sleep without, but it also gives us the chance to make some of the activities a bit more Beaver-friendly.

As I write this, we are planning our Summer camp in a couple of weeks, and we are going to do archery with the Cubs and Scouts. There is an age limit on that activity, so we've bought a couple of safe, sucker pointed archery sets and we're going to use them with the Beavers in the woods to do a "teddy bear hunt". That Idea was generated in a short whatsapp conversation between myself and Jim just last week!

I love the idea that the little red (and currently pristine) teddy bear that my 7 year-old son Thomas has decided is his camp mascot will be hanging off his backpack when he is on an expedition in the Borneo Jungle in 15 years time. Care-worn, falling apart, with little rips and stains, sewed up and even a little bit singed, it will tell the story of a Scouting life well lived, and a Scouting future full of promise.

Your own Scouting journey

I hope that you've enjoyed reading this book as much as I have enjoyed writing it. Hopefully it has given you a few ideas and ways of thinking that you might use to create magical experiences in your own group. I'd love to hear back about any of the ideas that you've used and changed for your own group. And any ideas that you think would be worth sharing with the wider Scouting community. My email is vm.jlouttit@Scouts.ie

Scouting is a wonderful lifelong activity. Whether you are just starting out on your journey, looking to re-invigorate your ideas, or just a deeply passionate Scouter who loves everything about what they do and likes to hear how other people do it, I want to thank you for reading this book. Giving up your time to help children have the amazing experiences Scouting can bring is an incredibly generous thing to do and you probably don't get thanked enough for it. I would like to add my voice to the voices of all those children, parents and other Scouters all over the world who should be singing your praises every day for the passion and energy that you put into this life-affirming organisation.

I wish you the very best with everything you do. Thank you and Happy Scouting!

James "Beaver Leader" Louttit

For lots of ideas and to join a community that is passionate about creating Brilliant Scouting, check out:
https://www.skool.com/brilliant-scouting-3743

If you loved this book – Please leave a review wherever you bought it from so others can find it too.

Printed in Great Britain
by Amazon